Girl Power

Girl Power

Making Choices & Taking Control

by Patty Ellis

Momentum Books, Ltd.

Cover design and illustration by Elaine Halleck

Manufactured in the United States of America

1996 1995 1994 5 4 3 2 1

Momentum Books
6964 Crooks Road, Suite 1
Troy, Michigan 48098
USA

ISBN: 1-879094-25-8

Library of Congress Cataloging-in-Publication Data

Ellis, Patty, 1949 -
Girl Power: making choices & taking control/ by Patty Ellis.
p. cm.
"Age level: 13-18; grade level: 7-12"--CIP data sheet.
ISBN 1-879094-25-8 : $9.95
1. Teenage girls -- United States -- Life skills guides. 2. Self-esteem in adolescence -- United States. I. Title.
HQ798.E45 1994
305.23'5--dc20 93-45566
CIP
AC

Dedication

Most of what I know about living, I have learned from
the wonderful women in my family
whose love and support ever surrounds me.

To them, I dedicate "Girl Power"...

My grandmother, Claudia

My mother, Flo

and my daughters,

Stephanie Ann and Hilary Faith

Table of Contents

Special Thanks

For a long time, it has been my dream to write a book for teenage girls - and now, here it is. Some very special people have been there throughout the process to offer guidance, expertise and support. So, I take this opportunity to send out a heartful of love and thanks to...

Martha Hancock, for the interest she took when my love and concern for teenage girls first began to take wing.

Marge Caldwell, for believing in me when I didn't know how to believe in myself.

Dr. Herb Again, for countless hours of "gabfest" and all the times he said, "You can do it!"

Terri Nogues, for the tireless days of work and creativity she so unselfishly gave to "Pink Flash" Seminars - may we never have to blow up another balloon.

Al Eicher, whose company distributes my "A Friend Like Patty" video series, for his mutual concern for young people and his faith in my message.

Bill Haney, my publisher, who believed in me and wasn't afraid to take the chance that teenage girls might actually be interested in reading a book.

Kyle Scott, my editor, for direction, patience and her calm assurances.

For longtime buddies, Lynnette Graef, Jane Caldwell and Brandi Beverly, who sweetly prodded me on each time they asked, "How's that book coming?"

Rita LaRue, another longtime bud, for copies, copies and more copies.

Diane Feiler, wonderful friend and brainy attorney, for legal advice and loving interest in all my ups and downs.

Carlene and Kimberly, my almost-daughters, who, since entering my life, have always warmly supported my efforts.

Dick Williamson, my daddy and the world's greatest source of "old sayings", for all those breakfast meetings chocked full of terrific stories and loving advice.

Barbara, my "middle" sister, who has always been an inspiration to me.

Claudia, my baby sister, for tons of encouragement, hours of re-reading the manuscript and for never hesitating to say, "This sounds a little strange - might want to try a re-write here."

And to my husband, Walter...my gift from God and the one who has made the REST of my dreams come true.

Section I

The most important person here is you

This book is especially for you . . . In fact, I wrote it with you in mind. You are the most important person who will ever read the words on these pages. And I hope you will find something new and wonderful to learn about yourself on every page. Mostly, I hope this book will make your life a little easier and help you escape some of the pain so many girls seem to live with these days.

I wish there had been a book like this for me when I was your age, but there wasn't. I had to learn most of what I have written here for you the hard way. Believe me, learning lessons about life by reading a book is much easier than learning them by making dumb mistakes. And even though most of us do make our share of dumb mistakes, it surely is a lot more comfortable to avoid them if at all possible.

Unfortunately, when we females make dumb mistakes, our lives really show it, and we often end up paying over and over and over again for the poor choices we've made. I would like for the choices you'll be making about your life and your future to be smarter than some of mine have been. I hope this book will help.

Happy reading . . .

One

It's time for change

It's not easy being a teenager . . . It never has been. And from the way things look, it's not going to get easy any time soon. The main problem with being a teenager is that this is the time in your life when you come face to face with the biggest change a human being goes through—the change from being a "child" to being an "adult." Or at least, that's the plan.

Your teen years are those incredible "in between" years sandwiched just to the right of childhood and slightly left of grown-up. And being caught in that never-never land between childhood and adulthood is no fun trip to the mall. It's a major happening in your life, full of trauma and confusion—kind of like buying your first bra.

Now, if you happen to be a teenage *girl* (which you probably are or you wouldn't be reading this book), you've really got your work cut out for you during this fascinating, but frustrating, time of life.

Being a teenage girl, especially these days, can be very

hazardous to your health and self-esteem, not to mention your future. If you don't have some very good information to guide you, plus a strong belief in your value as a person, you may find your life spinning out of control—which is exactly what's happening to more and more teenage girls every day. Very few girls are making it to adulthood without heartbreak and regrets, and many will carry around memories filled with ghastly scars for the rest of their lives.

But it doesn't have to be this way! Becoming an adult doesn't have to be your own personal episode of "Friday the 13th." Things can be changed. And that's what this book is all about.

"Change" is an exciting word ...

Some of the changes you are going through are easy to see—like the ones to your body, for instance. Remember how your body used to look before hair in the armpit and "super-absorbant maxi pads"? The word that comes to my mind is "straight." I don't think anything on my body had a curve to it until I was fifteen—except my hair, which I wished was straight. When I was young, I used to gaze into the mirror at my "straight" body and daydream about how I would look when I finally became a teenager. "Will I be beautiful?" I wondered. "Will I be shapely?" "Will I have hair on my upper lip?" It was agony.

And then there are those changes that don't show up so easily, like mood swings, and roller coaster emotions. One minute, life is rocking along A-okay and the next thing you know, everybody's getting on your nerves BIG-TIME.

And what about all the changes that are happening to your values and beliefs? Do you find you're suddenly not so sure of things you used to believe in with all your heart? Do you find yourself asking questions about things that never used to cross your mind—questions about right, wrong, sex, life and death? What does it all mean? And where do you fit in? Children never ask these questions, you know, and the fact that you are is one more way to know you're becoming an adult.

There is another change coming you may not have thought about yet. It's a very big change only you and your fellow teens can control. It is the change you and your generation will make to the future. After all, no group of teens has left the world exactly as they found it. They've all written their own stories on the pages of history. They have all made changes on this planet Earth. Sometimes these changes have been for the better, and sometimes for the worse.

Yes, change is happening. It's happening all around you, everywhere you look. It's an exciting time in your life.

Now it's your turn . . .

Now you get to travel this road called "Change." It's a road that can get scary, which is why a lot of people (not just teens) don't want to get near it. Cruising down this road to adulthood sounds about as exciting as a headache. After all, who wants to deal with all that getting older stuff?

One girl I met said, "I don't know why anybody would want to be an adult. They have so many problems." Well, no kidding. It takes real strength to travel this road and face all of the changes that happen when you leave childhood behind. It's the kind of strength some folks don't seem to have.

Too many of us grow up thinking that having sex with somebody, or learning to drive a car, or getting the latest hip hairstyle will make us adults. I'm afraid it's not quite that easy. Growing up means different things to different people, but, to all of us, it means being brave. And maybe this sounds weird, but growing up also means asking a lot of questions.

The only progress we humans have ever made happened because somebody, somewhere, stood up and asked a question. The question usually started with the word "Why?" "Why does it have to be this way?" "Why can't we try something else?" "Why can't things be better?" The people who ask these questions are some of the bravest people you could ever know, and, very often, they are teens. You will come a little closer to being an adult every time you ask, aloud or to yourself, "Why?"

Believe it or not, there are many of us over here on the adult end of the change who wish we could help make your travels down this road a lot easier; but we can't. All we can do is offer a little advice here and there and tell you stories about what it was like when we made our changes. We can't do much more than that because change is a journey every person makes alone.

I'll bet you've already had a few "suggestions" from well-meaning friends and relatives about how best to travel this road. Perhaps your Dad has said he could tell you the best route to take. After all, he's been there and no one could possibly know a better way. And isn't it just like a Mom to offer to ride along, just so you won't get too lonely. And, besides that, she'll bring a few snacks. You may have even had a teacher or two who wanted to point you in the right direction, or a grandparent who knew exactly which course you should take.

But I imagine that, like most teens before you, you've told them all, "No thanks. I need to do this by myself." And now you go about trying to find your own way, struggling down this unknown road. Good for you. You can make it. But you will need a very brave heart.

Brave hearts before us . . .

I love to read about women with brave hearts, women who have had the nerve to ask "why?" and the strength to fight for changes. One of my favorites is Eleanor Roosevelt—interesting lady. In fact, one of my dearest possessions is an old faded photo taken of my daddy in 1943. As a young Marine fighting in the South Pacific during World War II, he became very ill and was sent to a hospital in Australia. In the photo, standing beside his hospital bed, is Eleanor Roosevelt, who was the first lady at that time. She was there to visit and encourage our young soldiers who were so far away from home. Eleanor Roosevelt knew what it was to be brave, and she was a woman who fought for changes her entire lifetime. If it hadn't been for her and many other women like her, you and I wouldn't be where we are today.

It wasn't that long ago that a woman couldn't own land or a home or her own place of business. Women had no say in government and weren't even allowed to vote! There were very few jobs offered to women. And if a woman did have to work, she wouldn't be paid as much as a man who was doing the very same job.

My own mother, during her 40-year career in banking, felt the pain of watching young men *she* had trained be promoted to positions over her. Why would such an unfair thing happen? Because at that time many people believed women simply were not capable of being bank officers. Only men were believed to be qualified for such positions. But, Mom got 'em. She had become an executive vice-president by the time she retired and had written a college text on bank operations.

In years past, teenage girls didn't have the life you have today. Basically, they looked forward to one big event—getting married. And that usually happened by the time they were 14 or 15, quite often with their parents arranging the whole thing, including the choice of the groom. Once married, girls were expected to produce lots of babies—boy babies, if you please. After all, boys could do more work around the farm or ranch and, besides, girl babies just didn't bring the same honor to a father. Many families who had girl babies kept on having children in hopes a boy baby would show up one day.

Having lots of babies was considered the thing to do years ago and, since there were no handy-dandy methods of birth control on every corner, females had very little choice in the matter. Even when women were poor and hungry and their bodies worn out, they kept on having babies. Many of them died while trying to bring yet another child into this world.

In days past, a girl's entire life consisted of cooking, cleaning, sewing, and tending to children. I believe those are very noble and wonderful things to do. In fact, I have done them all myself. But when you dream of doing something else, you should have the freedom to follow your heart.

Stop for a moment and think of all the young girls who have lived before you, whose names you will never know and whose faces you will never see, who longed deep down inside themselves to do something wonderful and exciting with their lives. I wonder how different the world would be today had they been allowed to dream?

Eleanor Roosevelt once said, "The future belongs to those who believe in the beauty of their dreams." Women haven't always been allowed to dream, but *you* can dream. You can dream as big and as high as you dare, because back there, somewhere, someone demanded "Change!"

It's time for change . . .

For most people, the defining years of their "generation" were their teenage years. My parent's generation was the '40s and mine was the '60s—not that I actually feel the '60s were "mine." The '60s sometimes made me uncomfortable, but then a lot of people felt that way about the '60s.

I'm sure you've heard of my generation. We were quite loud. Many older people were convinced we were going to ruin the planet; we didn't, of course. And even though some people are saying the same thing about your generation, you won't ruin the planet either. But we did leave our mark on the planet—as will you, too.

Most of my generation had an absolutely grand time terrorizing our parents and any other adults who might have been close by. They looked at our mini-skirts, our long hair, and our "flower power" and were sure we'd all go mad. Our music was a little louder and our attitudes a little wilder than any generation before us. We decided "love" was the answer to all of life's problems and working for a living was a big waste of time. Some of us even managed to get to a place called "Woodstock" for a rock concert people still talk about today. We protested against our government's involvement in Vietnam and loudly demanded to know why our friends should have to die in a place we'd never heard of. Some of the boys burned their draft cards and some of the girls burned their bras. (I never burned any of my bras—mostly because I'd had to buy them with my own money and it seemed like such a waste.) Does it sound like we were a wild bunch of radicals? Well, most of us are now parents.

Some of our ideas in the '60s were great, and some probably stank. But we sure made changes. We believed bringing changes was our mission here on Earth, and we screamed and marched and protested, hoping and believing that changes would come.

Maybe it's hard for you to understand such strong desire to make things different. Maybe you think all of the changes that matter have already been made and that there is nothing left for your generation to be concerned about. Maybe you think things are sort of okay. If you believe life as we know it today needs no improvement, or if you think your generation of teenage girls has no causes to unite for, no reasons to rally, no battles to fight, no challenges to face . . . well, have I got news for you: Teenage girl of the '90s, WAKE UP! It's your turn now. And it's TIME FOR CHANGE.

What needs to be changed?

Well, let's start with the most obvious. If you're like most girls, you've already learned to judge yourself by how you look, how much you weigh, and what you wear.

Little girls are told from birth that they are to be pretty, and little boys are told to be strong. Isn't that interesting? Especially when you consider that "pretty" is an outside thing over which we have little control, while "strength" comes from inside us, from character and discipline. Little girls are given compliments and hugs when every curl is in place and their socks match their headbands. Little boys are rewarded when they are brave and fair. So tell me, who's being taught to love and respect themselves for what they are?

More than likely, you've had more comments made to you about your "darling dress" than about your personality, your brains, or your ability to take control of your life. Boys don't hear about their "darling clothes." They hear that if they are directed and determined enough they can do anything in life they want. They also hear about team spirit, sticking together, and all-for-one, one-for-all type stuff. Girls hear just the opposite.

Girls are taught to COMPETE with each other. They're taught to weigh less, dress better, have curlier hair, and carry a more expensive purse. After all, those are the things that really matter in life, aren't they? Your brain has already been fed thousands of commercials and advertisements telling you how you should look and what you should wear, and since none of us ever look like the people in commercials, most of us end up totally disgusted with ourselves. What a complete and total waste of our precious time!

In Chapter 2 you'll find out how to throw this kind of rotten thinking right out the window. Because, let's face it, IT'S TIME FOR CHANGE.

The boob tube and you . . .

Not long ago, a study looked at 200 prime-time television programs with a teenage girl in the cast. The study was done to find out how teenage girls are being portrayed on television. The results? In every program, the teenage girl was silly, giggly, and boy-crazy. She never had a serious conversation with an adult or showed any interest in school, her studies, or her future. She usually talked about boys or going shopping, or she had some silly remark to throw in about whatever issue was being discussed on the program. All the girls came across as "bimbos."

That's what television writers seem to think about teenage girls. So, tell me, girls. What do you think about television writers? I think they need to get to know some REAL teenage girls. I also think they need to decide whose side they're on. I mean, are they concerned about you and your future or not? After all, you are one of their biggest customers. Is it too much to ask that they give a little thought to how their programs may affect *your* life?

Television is a powerful medium. Nearly *everyone* watches TV. But in a country that has the largest teen pregnancy problem of any nation on earth, and with AIDS killing people right and left, don't you think it's time to cool it with some of this sex stuff on television? For instance, if you were to have a baby with no legal father, everyone would have a cow; but when Murphy Brown does it, her ratings go up. No wonder you're confused. I'M confused.

Maybe you can't change what's on TV, but you *can* change what you choose to watch and how you feel about what you do watch. No doubt about it, IT'S TIME FOR CHANGE.

These boys need to meet some REAL women ...

While we're on the subject of entertainment, let me tell you something interesting I've learned from girls just like you. I did a survey of 7,000 teenage girls and asked them their opinions about something of great interest to me—music. More specifically, I asked about rock and rap music. The question was, "Do you think most rock and rap music videos show females in a positive or negative way?" Notice, the question asks about "most" videos, not all.

Now, the answers I got on this one really surprised me. I thought the answers would be evenly divided on this question, with half saying videos show females in a positive way and the other half saying videos show females in a negative way—but I wasn't even close. No, it turned out *better* than that: Eighty-five percent of teenage girls just like you said, "Most rock and rap videos show females in a negative way!"

This is great! It means that girls just like you actually do see and understand for themselves how many of the rock and rap groups put down women with their music and their videos. Many of the groups show females as victims of sexual assault and violence, things to be used and thrown away. And it seems like every rock star has to have at least three or four women, one is never enough.

Maybe those guys have a problem with women. Maybe they don't know how to have a relationship with just one girl at a time. Maybe they have never learned how to treat a girl with respect and honor. Who knows?

There's one thing I do know, though, and it kind of

surprises me: Who spends the most money on rock and rap albums in this country? Teenage girls just like you! Teenage girls are the ones who're making those rock and rap guys (you know . . . those very guys who treat women so badly), wealthy. Do you want to get those guys' attention? Stop buying albums from the groups that show such little respect for females. Write to them saying, "I still love you and think you are the greatest thing since lipgloss, kissy, kissy, kissy, and when you start singing about how great we girls are, I'll start buying your stuff again. Until then, my extra cash is going toward new shoes."

You have the power to make changes happen, and IT IS TIME FOR CHANGE.

A history of pain . . .

Some of the changes we need are for problems that have been around for a long time—like sexual abuse. Females have been sexually abused forever, but it has always been one of those subjects no one talked about. That is finally changing, which means we are making some progress.

Our government tells us that one in every four girls in this country is sexually abused. But, according to the answers teenage girls like you gave on my survey, the real numbers may be even higher than that. (See survey, page 179.)

Sexual abuse comes in many forms. It can be as terrifying as rape or as quiet as a vulgar comment made to you by a boy walking past you in the hall at school.

Sexual abuse is one problem that will never be solved until each and every young girl understands what it is and what she can do to stop it.

After you've read Chapter 4, you'll have a better understanding of these things, and you will know IT IS TIME FOR CHANGE.

The greatest heartache . . .

Over one million teenage girls get pregnant every year in the United States—that's nearly 3,000 each day. In 1990, two-thirds of babies born to teens were born to unwed girls. As horrifying as those numbers are, the story doesn't stop there. For pregnancy is not an "event" that happens and then passes. The ripple effect of teen pregnancy goes on and on and on . . .

Two out of three girls who get pregnant will drop out of school. Only half of them will get a high school diploma and very few will go on to college.

Dropping out of school almost always ends in a life of poverty. Forty-six percent of white children, 67 percent of black children, and 70 percent of Hispanic children who live with single moms are poor.

We now have 1.3 million children living with teen mothers. Half of these children have no legal father. Where are all the "daddies"? Good question.

For far too long, teenage girls like you have faced the agony of teen pregnancy and the destruction it brings to their futures. Many girls have bravely faced it alone. Teen pregnancy has been like a thief robbing young women of the best years and most precious experiences of thier lives.

You deserve a better future, a better life. Chapter 7 will tell you how you can bring about changes to one of the saddest problems we face today.

The time is now . . .

Many things that touch your life every day as a teenage girl need to be changed. We will talk about more of them in the chapters to come, but "Girl Power" isn't going to leave you with a long list of all the problems you have to face. You are going to find on these pages ideas for solving those problems.

Sometimes bad things in life beat us down. But

"power" comes when we make the choice to CHANGE those bad things. And getting new and better information is what usually helps us decide to make changes in our lives.

People once thought the Earth was flat. They SWORE it was flat because that's what everyone had always said—"The Earth is flat." Then, one day, someone who seemed to know what he was talking about told them the Earth wasn't flat—it was round—so they all CHANGED their minds. The Earth didn't change; THEY changed because they received new and better information.

It is the same with you today. Everything you feel about yourself is based on information you've received from your parents, your family, your friends, your school, your religion, the movies, television, the society we live in, and on and on and on . . . From the beginning of your life you've been told things about yourself and your role as a female. "All the women in our family have huge thighs." "You are so artistic." "The world's most magnificent women wear Revlon." All of the things you have been told are now what you believe about yourself and your value as a person.

Do you believe most teenage girls receive good, positive, loving messages about their place in society? I don't. Even if you are fortunate enough to have a wonderful family that loves and supports you, there are too many others around telling you that you are not valuable—at least, not as you are. They're telling you to BE something else: prettier, sexier, taller, thinner, better dressed, more popular, smarter . . . and so on and so on and so on.

Now I think it's time for you to have some new information. I think it's time for you to hear that you are perfectly wonderful AS YOU ARE and that the only thing that really needs to be changed about you is the way you feel about yourself and your place in this world. And I believe that by the time you've finished reading the last chapter of this book you will know how to make those changes.

Do you believe it is time for change? Are you ready to learn how to accept yourself completely? Are you ready to stop trying to be someone else? Are you ready to feel good about YOU? Then start reading. AND LET THE CHANGES BEGIN!

Two

How you look

This chapter is not about how to be beautiful. God knows, you hear enough about that from television ads and teen magazines to make you gag. Anyway, you are already beautiful but you probably just don't know it yet, that's all. This chapter is about learning who you are, making the best of it, accepting the rest of it, and getting on with your life.

It sounds pretty simple, doesn't it? Well, since you may have already been convinced that your biggest value as a female lies in how you look, how you dress, and how much you weigh, it may be harder than I think for me to get this message across. But I'm going to try.

You will find that the people who work hardest at telling you "how you should look" are usually the same people who are trying to sell you some sort of product. You will also find that no matter how many of their products you buy and wear, you will always look like you.

So unless you learn NOW how to accept and like yourself, you will waste a lifetime (not to mention a fat chunk of money) trying to be someone else. And what a total waste that would be because being someone else is one thing you can NEVER do.

"Please, God, let us all be pretty . . ."

We look at people who are pretty and figure they just can't be like the rest of us. Surely they never have bad breath or walk out of the bathroom dragging toilet paper on their heels. Sometimes we love them and sometimes we hate them, but we always wish we could be more like them.

When I was modeling, I would look at some of the girls who were so beautiful I couldn't stand it, and I'd think, "What did their parents know that mine never heard about?" We all want to be pretty, but what does it really mean? After many years of thinking about that very question and talking to all sorts of girls, from the ones who thought they WERE pretty to the ones who were convinced they were NOT, I've come to a conclusion about what it means. It means you were born. That's it.

People who are pretty were born that way. It's one of life's little surprises that we have no control over. It's not an accomplishment, and it's not something you can earn or learn. It just happens. Being pretty doesn't mean you will be happy or find love or have a good life. It simply means you were born looking a certain way. It has never been, nor will it ever be, enough to make life worth a dang.

Maybe you don't see yourself as pretty and maybe you do. Either way, what you DO with your life will bring you happiness and joy, not what you see in the mirror.

Pretty by itself won't cut it, and I'll bet Marilyn Monroe would be the first to agree.

Uh, can someone define "pretty?"

I'm not sure I know what "pretty" is. Every time I think I've figured it out, someone up and changes the rules. First, it's straight hair, and then it's curly. One day it's "skinny," but the next time you turn around it's "healthy." Who knows anymore? I sure don't.

In the 1600s, most of the famous artists were busy painting women who seemed to have had no trouble getting three square meals a day—plus maybe a few snacks on the side. If you were to show Rubens—the most famous artist of that style—what we call "pretty" today, he'd think the poor girl was starving to death.

Do you ever dream of going to Hawaii? Well, in days of old, the most desirable women in Hawaii were the ones who weighed the most. Pass the pineapples, please.

In the late 1800s, teeny-tiny waistlines became the "look." Can you believe some women were so set on having one of those cute little 18-inch middles that they actually broke a few ribs to get there?

In the 1950s, big boobs and blonde hair were the ticket, so gals like Marilyn Monroe were a big hit. Females everywhere were out buying "falsies" to stuff down their bras in hopes that they, too, could look like Miss Chest.

Then along came the 1960s and an English model named Twiggy. Twiggy was built along the lines of your average toothpick, and it suddenly became very popular to be thin. Young women became obsessed with looking like pencils. And for a while there it really got pathetic.

Thin is not so hot these days. Today, it's concrete calves, bulging biceps, and pointed pectorals. Sorry, but you can count me out.

What I really want to know is, what's next? Will all "pretty" women be 9 feet tall? Will they have square heads or be orange? Excuse me, but isn't this all just too stupid?

Here you can make your own rules . . .

Have you ever stopped to ask yourself WHO decides what's "pretty" and what's not? So which geniuses are supposed to tell the rest of us what looks good and what doesn't? Could it be "fashion editors of magazines" or "clothes designers"? Maybe it's the "cosmetic companies" or "advertising agencies." Are these the little plotters and schemers who drive the rest of us up the wall with all their fashionable "do's and don'ts"? Yep, it's all of them. Every one of them makes his living by convincing us we don't look good enough. Somebody get a rope; I say we hang 'em all.

Do you want to know how they do it? Do you want to know how they manage to get us to jump through the hoop and spend all of our bucks on their cute and clever suggestions? Well, it's really pretty simple. People who sell us things know that we are all looking for "something," but we're not sure what that "something" is—we just know that we need it.

Since we've already been convinced that we aren't good enough as we are, we feel we need "something" else. Where do we find that "something" we are looking for? "Somewhere" else, of course. We think, "If I just looked like her . . ." "If only I had that body . . ." "If only I had her face . . ." "If only I had those clothes . . ." And we daydream about all the millions of changes that would ha ppen to us "if only . . ."

People who sell us things know about our search for that magic "something." They very cleverly hire models who just happen to have been born with the face or body we are all sure brings instant happiness, and they pay them buckets of money to hold up the tube of lipstick (or whatever) they want us to buy.

Eventually, we see the ad in a magazine or on TV and think to ourselves, "Oh boy, that's it. If I use that lipstick, I'll look just like her, and then I won't be ME anymore, and I'll find that SOMETHING I've been looking for." So we rush to the store as fast as our little legs can carry us, whip out our wallets and buy that tube of lipstick. We open it, smear it on, and sneak a quick look in the mirror. "Okay," we tell ourselves, "something should happen any minute now." So we wait and wait, but nothing changes. We're still plain ol' us wearing new lipstick.

When will we females ever learn to love and accept ourselves just as we are? No additions or attachments necessary. Just as we are. Period. When will we learn to simply wear lipstick because it's what WE want to do (if indeed that IS what we want to do), and not because we think it will transform us into someone else?

Be different. Choose your own kind of beauty. Do what works for you and let the fashion editors hang. I think you're going to like this chapter—because it's going to tell you how.

It's all a picture ...

When people look at you, they see a picture. They don't see the real you. They see hair, a face, clothes, and a body—a picture of what you want or don't want them to see. They don't see the real, thinking, talking, hoping, dreaming, searching you. And unless they get the chance to really know you, all they will ever see is only a picture.

Now, most of us believe this picture is very important. In fact, for many of us, it's THE most important thing in life. If the picture is looking good, hot dog! We believe our picture makes us special and gives us value. It's where we place an awful lot of our time and energy—And a BUNCH of our cash.

And why shouldn't we? Most of us have been told since the day we were born that our picture is extremely important. We've been patted on the head when the picture was a pleasing one, and laughed at and made fun of when it was not. No wonder we females grow up believing how we look is the most important thing about us. No wonder we believe that if we can just be pretty enough, wear cute clothes, and have a good body we will find complete happiness AND the perfect man. Well, amigas, it's a lie.

By the time most of us figure out the message is a lie, we've already wasted 20 or 30 years—and sometimes an entire lifetime. When we believe how we look is the most important thing about us but aren't happy with how we look, what next?

We call it "low self-esteem." We begin seeing ourselves as not good enough, not measuring up to everyone else, not able to compete, and not worth much.

Well, we've believed this lie too long. We're smarter than this! It's time for change.

Don't much care for your picture?

I know you may not be completely happy with your own picture much, or perhaps even most, of the time. You may have already toyed with the idea of covering it with a sheet for the rest of your life. Nearly every girl, if perfectly honest, would like to change something about her picture—like maybe the whole, entire thing. We'd all probably like to change our own pictures.

Unfortunately, we can't do that. Our mothers met our fathers and fell in love. After a while, here we came. What you see is what you get. It would have been very nice had your parents handed you a "Looks Order Form" eight or nine months before you were born so that you could choose your future bod. You could have had such fun checking the little squares beside the multiple choices. "Let's see . . . I'll take this hair, these eyes, that face, this body, those legs, these boobs and, oh, how about those teeth?"

Wouldn't that have been fabulous? And no more dirty dishes would be great, too, but life doesn't work that way. We are not products of "Make A Wish." Each of us is a product of "genes," donated by Mom, Dad, Grandma, Grandpa, and all the other squirrels in the family tree.

So here you are. Physically, very little of what you are is ever going to change, unless you happen to be Michael Jackson and really dig cosmetic surgery. And since most of us are not Michael Jackson, we may as well make the most of what we've been given, even if it isn't exactly what we want.

First, forget about "perfect"...

There are no perfect people. There are no perfect faces. There are no perfect bodies. There are people, faces, and bodies that someone else THINKS are perfect. But, that's just a mere opinion.

I've seen the painting of the Mona Lisa. Some people say she's perfect. She didn't look perfect to me, nor has anyone else I've ever laid eyes on—except my own two daughters. That's my opinion, of course. There are probably many people who don't think my two daughters are perfect, which only proves my point.

"Beauty is in the eye of the beholder." That's an old saying, which means we all see beauty in our own special places. Personally, I'm sick and tired of being told where to see it, and I want you to get tired of it, too. I want you to open your eyes and see your own beauty. You are one of a kind, special, and different.

Besides, who really cares who's on the cover of Seventeen this month?

Here it comes . . .

On the next few pages, you'll read about the four steps to becoming happy with your body picture. These steps aren't difficult; in fact, they are quite simple. But they won't do you a bit of good unless you really use them. I use them constantly. And they work.

Step 1: Take a long and honest look at yourself . . .

We look at everyone else in the world except the one person we should be looking at most closely—ourselves. We look at other girls, the models pictured in our favorite magazines, our friends . . . and THEN we decide how we should look.

This is crazy. Comparing yourself to someone else is the biggest waste of time in the universe. What difference does it really make in your life how someone else looks? What should matter to you is how YOU look. So, how do you look?

Below are a few questions that will help you understand your body and looks a bit better. This isn't something you can pass or fail. It's simply for your own information.

First, look honestly at the shape of your body.

Are you . . .

Petite?	Large?
Tall?	Short?

Do you have . . .

Long legs?	Short legs?
Long arms?	Short arms?
Long waisted?	Short waisted?
Narrow hips?	Wide hips?
Narrow shoulders?	Broad shoulders?

Small feet?	Large feet?
Long neck?	Short neck?
Large hands?	Small hands?
Large breasts?	Small breasts?

There is no "right" or "wrong" way to be, but making the most of your body picture first requires an honest understanding of what it is.

What is the shape of your face? Is it . . .
Round?
Long?
Square?
Oval?

Is your face widest at the . . .
Jaw?
Forehead?
Cheekbones?

Look closely at your own face in the mirror. What is the shape of your nose? How far apart are your eyes? Are your eyelashes long or short? Are your eyebrows thick? Would you describe your eyelids as small or large? Is your forehead long or short?

What type of complexion do you have? Skin comes in many different hues and three shades—light, medium, or dark. Your complexion is the shade of your skin color. My skin is white, and my complexion is very, very light. (I've been mistaken for a ghost on several occasions.) My friend Valerie is black, and her complexion is medium. Knowing your complexion is very important when choosing cosmetics.

How would you describe your hair? What color is it? Is it . . .
Thin?
Thick?

Coarse?
Fine?
Curly?
Wavy?

"Thick" and "thin" have to do with how much hair is actually growing on your head. Do you have wads of hair or just a strand here and there? "Coarse" and "fine" have to do with the size of each strand. In other words, is a hair from your head fat or skinny? You can have thick, fine hair; thin, coarse hair; or thick, coarse hair. Isn't this fun? (I can almost hear you saying "Like, who cares?" But, listen: This is not really as dumb as it sounds.)

When you've answered all these questions, you'll have a pretty good idea of what you have to work with in your very own picture. The answers will help you choose clothing styles, cosmetics, and hair styles. And until you've answered these questions about yourself, you may waste a lot of time and money buying the wrong things.

Someone once told me that the best way to take an honest look at yourself is to put a paper bag over your head (with two eye-holes cut out) and stand nude in front of a mirror. I've never quite found the nerve to try it. (I'm afraid one of my kids would walk in and decide I had finally gone completely mental.) But whatever works for you is okay by me. Know thyself. Thou art worth knowing. (You can call me Shakespeare if you like.)

Step 2: Change what you can . . .

When you take a long, honest look at yourself, you'll probably find a few things you're not so crazy about. It's okay; that's life. Remember: Nobody in this universe is perfect. Before you decide to chuck your whole body into the nearest river, why not look at the things that can be changed?

Let's start with your hair. With cuts, perms, straighteners, lighteners, mousses, and gels, hair hardly has to be "what you see is what you get" anymore. I can't imagine what women used to do *without* all of these products. They must have worn a lot of hats, I guess. Teenage girls are always first in line to try fun, new hair styles and products. And that's great. Too many women, as they get older, lock themselves into a hairstyle and hang on to it for dear life. (That's one of the reasons they may start to look so ancient before their time.) Have fun with your hair and don't be afraid to make changes.

Another thing that can be changed is your weight, but we'll talk about that later on in this chapter.

Exercise can change your body—it can build it up and tone it down. Remember, the changes that exercise brings happen very slowly, so be patient. Don't expect to do one sit-up and see a different person in the mirror the next morning.

Something as simple as a good manicure and a coat of polish can change the look of your hands—and feet, which need all the help they can get. Cosmetics can make some of the biggest changes in how we look, and we'll talk about them in the next few pages.

In short, there *are* things about your body picture that *can* be changed. It's up to you.

Step 3: Accept what you cannot change . . .

Sometimes, when we look in the mirror, we see things about ourselves we decidedly do NOT like. Here is where we can get a little crazy. We figure that PART of ourselves is pretty crummy. Then we spot someone whose PART looks better than our PART. "Her PART looks good." "My PART looks sick." CONCLUSION: "She is better than me!" Well, this is nuts.

You are worth more than just a bunch of spare PARTS.

You are a whole person whose parts go together to create someone who is unlike any other. I have a set of legs any donkey would be proud to own. And every time I see my mother's legs (and the legs of several of my aunt's when we're together at family reunions), I know exactly where these two miracles of nature came from. So, what am I supposed to do, have leg transplants?

Hardly. I merely need to accept the fact that I cannot change my legs. They walk, cross, dance, skip, and carry me to work, for goodness sake. So what if nobody is asking me to do hosiery commercials? Does this mean I'm not as valuable a person as the girl who does them? No, it just means that she was born with great leg genes and I wasn't.

Am I really supposed to go through my life believing that some girl who happens to have been born with gorgeous legs is better than me? *No way.* (How I wish someone had told me this when I was in junior high. Maybe then I wouldn't have wasted so much time hating myself every time I saw Becky Green's beautiful legs.)

Step 4: Make the most of what you've got . . .

If I showed up to speak at your school one morning still wearing my favorite pink terry cloth robe, with no makeup and with my hair fresh off the pillow, I'll bet you'd be shocked. It wouldn't matter how many great points I made or how many funny stories I told. No one would hear me. Who's going to listen to some nutcake standing in front of the student body in her bathrobe?

Even the most glamorously beautiful women in the world (a group, alas, which does not include me), have to get up and get it together at some point during the day. No one bops out of bed in the morning looking terrific. Remember, "terrific" doesn't mean "born beautiful." Terrific means learning who and what you are and making the most of it.

When you see someone who looks great, you can bet she has given a lot of thought to her appearance and has spent time and energy to present her best face to the world. The most attractive women, young or old, are always the ones who've learned how to make the most of what they've got.

Making all this work for you . . .

Now you know the four steps that will help you become happy with your body picture. Let's look at them again . . .

1. Take a long, honest look at yourself.
2. Change what you can.
3. Accept what you cannot change.
4. Make the most of what you've got.

Now, it's time to put these steps to work.

Most of us hope someone will come along and tell us how to look our very best. We figure we could never do this for ourselves, but we can. Unless you reach Hollywood someday and receive "star" treatment, you will have to do it for yourself. The advice on these pages will give you the main facts you need to start making your picture one you can be happy with. From there, it's up to you.

I'm going to divide this advice into three parts: Clothes, hair, and cosmetics. I want you to think about *yourself* as you read these pages. Don't think about your best friend or the girl at school whose looks you envy. You are the one I'm talking to. Make it work for YOU.

But I don't have a thing to wear . . .

When it comes to your clothes, ask yourself the following questions:

1. How do I LOOK when wearing certain styles and colors? Don't be afraid to judge yourself. Open your eyes and look at yourself in a mirror. Do you like what you see? Or does something look "wrong?" If something looks wrong, ask yourself what it is. Is it the style, the length, the color, or the way the clothes fit? You've got a good brain and good eyes—use them.

2. How do I FEEL when wearing different styles and colors? Have you ever noticed that when you wear a certain color you feel like death warmed over? That's me in pale pink. If you feel crummy when you wear yellow or feel like a moose when you're in shoulder pads, then pay attention to those feelings. Why do you feel like a million dollars whenever you wear your red dress? Learn to trust your own feelings about the clothes you wear.

3. What comments do I hear when wearing different styles and colors? I would be the last person in the world to suggest you dress to suit other people, but paying attention to their reactions can help you know things about yourself you can't see. For instance, if people keep asking if you've read the newest diet book by Dr. Nofat Nomoah every time you wear that pink dress, BURN it. Do you get compliments each time you wear your dark green blouse? Then dark green must be your color. Keep an eye open for dark green items—on sale, of course. Notice the things you're wearing when you receive the most compliments about your appearance. Then ask yourself why.

Now, with those three questions in mind, think about the styles you buy. Most of us are so busy trying to keep up with the latest fad, we never stop to think whether it really looks good on us. We waste a lot of money buying the wrong things. I'll bet you have things in your closet right now that you never wear because, once you bought them and brought them home, you realized they were not right for you. But it was too late because you were stuck with them, right? Let's see if we can't be smart enough to keep that from happening again.

Read the following list and ask yourself which looks best on your own picture:

Short skirts	Long skirts
Belts	Loose waistlines
Shoulder pads	Natural shoulder line
Long jackets	Short jackets
High collars	Little or no collar
Long sleeves	Shorter sleeves
Dark colors	Bright colors
Fitted pants	Fuller cut pants
Loosely-fitted clothes	Form-fitting clothes

In some cases, you may be able to wear either selection.

If you're not sure, the next time you have a little extra time on your hands, head for the mall and try on some of the different styles listed here. Look closely at your image in the mirror—from the back, sides and front. Be your own best judge. Once you begin to pay close attention to how you look when wearing different styles and colors, it should be quite easy to see what works best for you.

Before we leave this section on clothes, there is one more teeny thing I'd like to mention: WHAT you wear speaks about the person you are. And this has nothing to do with brand names. Not long ago I was in an airport and a young girl walked through the terminal wearing high heels, very tight shorts, and a halter top. She caught the eye of everyone in the place—especially the men. I couldn't help but notice, as she walked by, how the men would look her up and down, make some sort of remark to each other, and then die laughing. Maybe they were commenting about how much she looked like their dear, sweet grandmothers, but I doubt it. And maybe she didn't really care what they were saying about her, but I did. It made me angry. I don't know why men can act like animals sometimes, but our strutting around in front of them half naked doesn't help the situation. Now, I know you're a big kid now and can wear anything you please—as long as your Mother doesn't catch you. But, don't kid yourself.

HOW you dress speaks very loudly about WHO YOU ARE. That girl in the airport may have been studying to become a nun, but I don't think anyone else in the airport that day would have guessed it. Rock video bimbettes wear transparent clothing and live to tell the story, but the minute you try walking around in one of those outfits, you'll have a king-sized sleazeball trying to claim you for his own. And then you may have more trouble on your hands than you can handle.

As women, we've fought long and hard for our "rights." And, okay, so wearing as little as possible may be one of our "rights"—but it should be something we save for the "right" time and the "right" guy. When you truly value yourself, you don't put everything you have on display for any jerk who comes along to see and make nasty little comments about. You're worth more than that.

Hair today and still hair tomorrow . . .

Isn't hair interesting? It just sits there on top of your head serving no real purpose, other than to drive you mad. The big problem, of course, is finding the best way to wear it. I admit, this is no small feat.

Before you can begin to find the right hairstyle for yourself, you must first decide which type of hair you have. In "Take a long and honest look at yourself," I asked if your hair is thick, thin, coarse, or fine. Obviously, if your hair is thick, certain styles will suit you better than if it is thin. And, if your hair is fine, it will style much differently than if it is coarse.

Now that we have that out of the way, the big question is: "How do I find the right hairstyle?"

Following these suggestions should help.

1. Choose a style you like. I know this sounds too simple, but it's the most basic place to start. Don't waste your time with a hairdo that doesn't please you. Look at magazines and TV ads for something that catches your eye. Find the "do" you want.

2. Choose a style that is right for your hair type. The questions you've just answered about your hair will help you to find a style that suits you best. It is pointless for me to try to wear one of those cute, straight "bobs," chopped off bluntly at the ends. I love that look, but my hair is thick, coarse, and curly, so there's no way. Find what works best for you.

3. Choose a style you can fix all by yourself. If YOU can't make it look good, what's the point? Unless you live at a beauty salon, it's important to find a hairstyle that you can keep without too much strain on your nervous system.

4. Choose a style that fits your lifestyle. Are you on the swim team and spend half your life in the water? Long hair will be a pain. Find a style that makes you comfortable and fits the way you live. I travel a lot and can't stand the thought of spending much time fooling with my hair, so I wear it short. It's easy to keep and quick to fix.

5. Choose a style that matches your body. If you are tiny, don't wear a huge hairdo. On the other hand, if you're large, don't wear a teeny tiny hairdo. If you're tall and thin, don't wear loooong, straaaight hair. And if you're petite, leave the beehives alone.

After you have chosen a hairstyle you think you can live with and are ready to go for it, what do you do? My all-time, number one suggestion at this point is to GET YOURSELF A GOOD HAIRCUT. You may save a few dollars by having your best friend's cousin the tree trimmer give it a whack, but you probably won't look so great. I'm all for saving money, but, this is one place NOT to scrimp.

How do you find a good hairstylist?

1. Look around. Talk to girls who have great-look-

ing hair and ask them where they have it done. They will love that you asked and will probably go on and on until you absolutely want to throw up.

2. Never look for a doctor or a hairstylist in the Yellow Pages. One could kill you and the other might just make you want to kill yourself.

3. When you go in for your appointment, TALK to the stylist before she (or he) begins working on you. Tell her what you want. Show her pictures, drawings, or whatever it takes to get the message across. Don't assume she'll know what you're after. Most hairstylists aren't mind readers. Don't be afraid to speak up. If your stylist acts as though she doesn't want to talk to you, jump out of the chair and run as fast as you can.

Now at this point I could give you pages and pages of "tips" on hair care, but you can read all about that in the next issue of your favorite teen magazine. And, anyway, that's not the purpose of this book. I wrote this book to help you learn how to like yourself for what you are (split ends and all), make the best of what you've got, and get on with what's really important in your life.

We females waste so much time fretting and fussing over our hair. Yet, in spite of all our fretting and fussing, our hair just continues to be itself, never seeing things our way and always proving to us we can't really change it. If we can learn to accept our hair, we are well on our way to accepting all the other parts of ourselves—even the ones we don't happen to like.

Just a dab here and a smidge there . . .

Did you know that cosmetics are the second biggest purchase made by teenage girls? (The first is clothing—big shock.) In fact, girls your age use more eyeliner, eyeshadow, lipgloss, mascara, and nail polish than adult women do. And they buy more shampoo, conditioner, and hair spray. Women, young and old, spend billions of dollars on cosmetic products each year.

Unfortunately, most of us are wasting our money, because having that "flawless-finish" look has nothing to do with paying big bucks.

Let's say you spot a girl whose makeup is perfect. Can you tell simply by looking at her whether she is wearing expensive, department store makeup, or less expensive products from a drug or discount store? Of course you can't tell, but most of us think that to look good we have to buy the big name brands we see advertised. We end up spending a lot of money we don't have trying to get something they can't give us.

Not that there is anything wrong with the expensive cosmetic lines. They're wonderful, but you certainly don't need to buy them to look fabulous. You see, there are only so many basic ingredients in any cosmetic. For instance, if you add many more things to an eyeshadow, it's not an eyeshadow anymore—it's cornbread.

Don't be fooled by fancy packages and slick sales tricks that try to convince you beauty can be found in a jar. It's just not true. Eyeshadow is eyeshadow, whether you pay $2 or $20. It's fine if you have $20 to pay for eyeshadow, but, once you get it on, no one will be able to tell it cost so much.

You can get great cosmetics without spending your last dime. For instance, Lancome and L'Oreal are made by the same company, Cosmair. The main difference between the two products is that Lancome costs much more, has fancier packaging, and is sold in big department stores; L'Oreal is cheaper, not so fancy, and sells at the drug stores. They have the same basic quality but sell at different prices. Look for *me* at the drug store.

The same is true of Revlon. You can buy Natural Wonder Foundation makeup by Revlon for less than $4 at most drug or discount stores, or you can pay about $30 for Revlon's Ultima Foundation at a department store. Once it's on, I can't tell the difference. So, where would you rather spend your money? I'd rather save mine for a '57 T-Bird convertible.

Great makeup depends on how well you apply it, not what you pay for it. Don't ever forget it.

I guess the most important advice I can give to you about makeup is this: Wear some, but not too much. A few years ago, some of the women who were trying to prove they could get out there and make it in a man's world decided they shouldn't wear makeup at all. I guess they thought they should look "natural," like the men. That was silly. Who in the world wants to look like a man?

Makeup helps you look your best, no doubt about it. And looking your best is a super way to show the confidence you feel in yourself. That kind of confidence will carry you a lot further in life than trying to be one of the guys.

Wearing makeup well is an art. It requires practice and patience. It also requires learning who YOU are and what looks good on YOU. Your makeup needs are as one-of-a-kind as the rest of you, so find what works for you—experiment, be creative, and look fabulous. Just don't get so interested in how good you look that you forget the important things -- like going to college!

Remember what we decided about "perfect"?

Teen magazines are fun, and they're a great place to find tips on the latest trends in makeup, clothing, and accessories. They also have good articles on skin care, diet information, and exercise programs. Looking at the pictures of the models will give you super ideas about your own makeup and hairstyles. Once in a while they even have sensible articles on issues that are important to you.

Overall, teen magazines are a pretty good source of ideas, if you can deal with all the "too-cute" stuff. It can be very depressing to look at the nauseating pictures of the "perfect" girls, with their "perfect" hairstyles and wearing "perfect" clothes and sitting in their "perfect" rooms—gag. Remember what we decided about "perfect?" It doesn't even exist.

Here's an idea. . . . Maybe someday you'll become an owner or an editor of a teen magazine and insist on showing a more honest view of what it's like to be a REAL, LIVE, teenage girl. What a change that would be!

Beauty is where you find it . . .

One of the most beautiful young women I have ever known is not thin. She is what most of us would call overweight. But, she is beautiful. Her skin is gorgeous. Her hair is the latest. Her makeup is flawless. And she knows how to wear the right clothes for her body—flowing but not too loose. She wears large jewelry, has perfect posture, carries herself like a queen and always smells divine.

All of the girls around her want to know her makeup secrets, who does her hair, where she shops and whether she can come to the mall and help them shop. Everyone loves her. Beauty is not found in what you weigh, it's found in what you are.

Do you really NEED to lose weight?

So, now let's talk about the dreaded subject that gets an awful lot of attention these days - weight!

But first, for those of you who just moaned, "do we really HAVE to?", a question: Do you NEED to lose weight? I mean, do you REALLY need to lose weight, or are you being tempted to judge yourself by someone else's picture?

Stop for just a moment, here, and concentrate only on yourself. Think about your height, your bone structure, the build of your body and the size and build of the people in your family. Think about how you look in your clothes. Are you usually pleased with how you look when dressed up? (Forget about how you look when you are NOT clothed - there's not one in a million of us who is happy with that sight.) Does your weight affect your day-to-day living? In other words, are you out of breath after walking up a flight of stairs or do you find yourself not participating in sports or other activities because your weight limits you? Giving some thought to these things can help you discover whether or not you NEED to lose weight.

The belief that they are "too fat" is causing tremendous pain in the lives of many girls today. And that pain and confusion about how their bodies should look often results in broken health and even death. Let's talk about ANOREXIA NERVOSA and BULIMIA.

The typical anorexic girl is one with an obsession for becoming thin who will starve herself on as little as 100 calories per day. She believes she can gain control over her life and win approval of others if she can only be thin enough. Without treatment, the anorexic girl could possibly starve herself to death.

The bulimic will eat incredible amounts of food at one sitting (called binging) and then try to get rid of all she has eaten or "purge" herself by vomiting or taking laxatives. Bulimia can also result in serious health problems, even death.

If you suffer from or have even considered trying either of these eating disorders, please find someone to talk with IMMEDIATELY! These are extremely serious matters which can ruin your health and even your life.

Remember that the question before you in this section is: Do you really NEED to lose weight? This is a question no one can answer but you. And before we go any further with our discussion of weight, it is one I would like for you to think about in a very personal way.

Do you really WANT to lose weight?

If the answer to the above question is "yes", then let's get the excuses out of the way.

It is possible to lose weight. In fact, if you do certain things, it is impossible NOT to lose weight. If you cut down on the calories or fats entering your body and you begin a wise and steady exercise program, you will lose weight. Anyone who maintains a high weight but continues to say, "I never eat a thing" is not being honest with themselves. You CAN'T "not eat a thing" and stay overweight. It is humanly impossible. The body can only grow when fed - stop feeding it and there is no way it will continue to grow larger.

The main reason I know it is possible to lose weight is because so many people do it. If it was impossible, no one would have ever done it!

The reason I am making such a large deal of this is because I believe with every ounce of my being that it is impossible to solve ANY problem in life without first being honest about it. Whether the problem be weight, abuse, drugs or whatever, it must be faced before it can be fought. Too many of us make excuses about our weight rather than doing something about it. We whine and moan to anyone who will listen that we are "fat" but never seem to be able to take control and change that part of ourselves.

If you have answered "yes" and feel you need to shed some pounds, then let's find a way to do it! But, if you feel you don't really need or want to lose weight, quit talking about it! Don't feel that you have to act like you want to be skinny if you're happy as you are. Instead, shock everyone you know with a dose of your healthy self-love by claiming, "I like me the way I am."

Remember, if you want to lose weight, you CAN. It is NOT impossible.

Broccoli and brussel sprouts . . .

What is impossible, though, is to lose weight while eating the typical teenage diet. Most teenage girls are not into broccoli, and that's too bad. Broccoli is one of the best foods you can eat. It has very few calories and is great for you. Corndogs and strawberry shakes, on the other hand, are another story.

Many people believe that if you are overweight, you must be eating like a horse—not true. A huge appetite usually is not the problem with weight control. The big problem is WHAT you eat. You can have all the carrots, apples, cucumbers, and grapefruit you want and not be bothered with weight gain, unless of course we're talking tons of carrots here. It's when you are having sweet rolls and chocolate milk for breakfast, a bacon cheeseburger and large fries for lunch, pizza for dinner, and chips and cokes in between that you'll find yourself growing larger by the minute.

If you really want to lose weight, the first thing you probably need to do is take a close look at what you feed yourself. A slice of pizza now and then isn't going to kill anybody, but if you only eat foods handed to you from a drive-through window, you may want to make some changes. And today is a great time to start.

You CAN, but . . .

You have very little say about two things that greatly affect your weight. You will notice that I said "affect" and not "control." You "control" your weight.

First, there are those ghastly little "genes." Blame your family for this one. If most of them tend to be short and stocky, you probably won't ever be a 5'9" beanpole. If you look closely at the members of your family you will see parts of yourself in all of them.

Second is a thing called "metabolism." Metabolism is the way your body takes in and burns up the food you feed it. Girls with high metabolisms are the ones who seem to eat everything in sight and never gain an ounce. Low metabolism means you barely look at a piece of chocolate cake and you blow up like a helium balloon.

Now, both genes and metabolism are important to think about when you decide to lose weight. They both have a lot to do with how easy or difficult it may be.

Losing weight is like getting an education. We can all do it, but some of us have to work a lot harder than others.

A body care plan for life . . .

You could spend the rest of your life going on diets—which is what many women do. But what would be better by far is to change your way of thinking. You can be among the first generation of women who start as teens to take control of their bodies and health simply by being smart about eating, what and how much, and about exercise. This would be far better than buying into all of those "quick and easy" diet plans. Taking good care of your body is a choice you make every day of your life. It's a choice only you can make.

My Lifetime Body-Control Plan is the plan I live by. It is not a one-time diet you follow for a few weeks to lose weight and then forget. It is an ATTITUDE—an attitude about how much you value yourself as a person. If you will follow the 20 steps you are about to read, you can begin to control your weight today, and never let it control you.

Introducing "Patty's Lifetime Body-Control Plan" . . .

Remember, YOU are the important person here. Think only of yourself as you read this plan, not your best friend, not the model you wish you could be—only you! The first 11 steps should be used all of the time. They will keep you and your body in good shape and help you learn that "control" we've been talking about. The last 9 steps are for you to use when you want to lose weight. As you read each of these steps, think of how they can work for you. You have already learned how to accept yourself for what you are, now let's make that person the best she can be.

1. EXERCISE

Start an exercise program today. This is a must. Exercise at least three or four times each week (more if you are really determined to get in shape). Walk, swim, jog, skate, play tennis, golf, or do aerobics with friends—but do SOMETHING. Turn off the TV, get up off that sofa, and DO IT! I do water aerobics 30 minutes a day, 4 days a week, and, as Joe Piscopo says, "Not for vanity, but for sanity." Exercise clears your mind and gives you a mental lift that you can't get anywhere else. Go for it!

2. LEARN EVERYTHING YOU CAN ABOUT FOODS

A banana split will put more weight on you than a banana. Maybe you know this and maybe you don't. It's not something you are born knowing. You must learn these things. There are great books and good articles in the newspaper every day that tell you everything you need to know about food and what it does to your body.

Once you begin to learn about foods, you may be surprised. For instance, many girls think a baked potato is fattening, but it's not the potato that's the problem, it's all of the junk we put on it—like the sour cream, the bacon and the cheese (tasty, sure, but loaded with fat). The foods you give your body will determine how healthy and strong you will be. This is one place where it pays to be choosey.

3. EAT YOUR FRUITS AND VEGETABLES

Fruits, vegetables, and grains alone could sustain us and keep us healthy, but we often give in to that urge to dig into a juicy hamburger. You may like some fruits but think vegetables stink. Sorry, but you'll never be in control of your body with that attitude. You CAN find vegetables to like, but you may have to open your mind to new tastes. Some girls tell me they refuse to eat anything that has ever been in the dirt. Puh-leeze! Fruits and vegetables are the very best food you can feed your body. Try salads, but go easy on the salad dressing.

4. CHOOSE WHOLE GRAIN BREADS AND CEREALS

You know how kitchen sinks can get all clogged up sometimes by all that fat and grease and stuff? Well, the very same thing happens to you—you can get clogged up—when you load up on Miss Fruity Sugar Pellets or nothing but white bread sandwiches. Along with fruits and vegetables, whole grain breads and cereals give our systems the roughage it needs to stay cleaned out and healthy. Become a label reader and find out what's in the breads and cereals you eat. Look for things like whole grains and high fiber—like whole wheat, oats, and barley—and be sure to watch out for fat and cholesterol.

5. GO EASY ON THE FRIED FOODS

Fried foods are the kiss of death when it comes to body control. They are not good for your skin, weight, or general health. Did you know that eating an average sized portion of chicken-fried steak, gravy, and an order of fries is the same as eating one and a half sticks of butter? Think of all that fat clogging up your body, not to mention what it does to your hips. Check out the fat content of your favorite chips, too.

6. ABOUT THOSE MILK PRODUCTS

If you are a milk drinker, make it low-fat. Two percent milk has less fat than whole milk, and skimmed has even less. If you like cottage cheese or yogurt, try the low-fat kinds. And if you are an ice cream nut, low-fat frozen yogurt is yummy and will satisfy your sweet tooth without all of the calories.

7. LEARN TO COUNT CALORIES

Even though I'm not on a diet, I constantly watch what I eat. And an easy way to do that is to count calories. A calorie is a unit of energy. Your body burns a certain amount of calories each day. If you take in more calories than you burn, you will probably put on weight. We all need some kind of system to help us keep track of what we eat. When you are young and don't understand all of the confusing details about food, counting calories is a simple way of keeping score.

8.GET A GOOD CALORIE-COUNT BOOK

You can find these little books in any bookstore and most grocery stores. (Check with your mother—she probably has 15 or 20 of them already.) One book I recommend is Jean Carper's "THE ALL IN ONE CALORIE COUNTER." It's great because it gives the calorie count not only for all your favorite fastfoods, but also for many prepared foods you find in the grocery store.

9. DON'T BE CRUEL TO YOURSELF

Everyone deserves a candy bar now and then, but here is where your control can go out the window. If you find yourself craving a Snicker's, go ahead. But try to eat the small size bar or only a few bites of the large size and then put the rest away for later. I am very careful about what I feed myself, but once in a while I have to have a donut or I'll die. Dolly Parton says she lost weight by eating just a bite of everything she wanted. YOU are in control of your body. Don't let your cravings control YOU.

10. WATER IS A MUST

Drink lots and lots of water. It's good for your body and great for your skin. Over ice and with a straw helps me.

11. DON'T GO HOURS WITHOUT FOOD

It's not good for you to go for long periods without

food and your energy will hit bottom if you do. It's much better to snack often than to let yourself get so hungry you start inhaling food like a human vacuum cleaner. But keep "good" snacks around, like grapes, bananas, apples, oranges, carrot sticks, and low-fat frozen fruit bars. Keep a large pitcher of your favorite diet drink ready in the fridge. Sugar-free drinks by Crystal Light, Country Time, and Kool-Aid are super and much cheaper than diet soft drinks.

As I said before, there 11 steps should be part of your daily life. If you need to lose weight, add the following steps to your routine:

12. TELL YOURSELF YOU CAN

Don't ever say "I can't lose weight" or "I'll always be fat" again. You DO have control over your diet and your weight—believe it!

13. FORGET ABOUT "EASY"

There is no such thing as "easy" weight loss. Pounds go on one at a time, so they have to come off the same way. Once you have gained weight, losing it is a long, hard job, but you CAN do it.

14. DO IT FOR YOU

Take control of your weight for YOU, not so you will get a boyfriend or so you can be like someone else. Do it for YOU. Believe in YOU. Know that YOU will look and feel better if you take control of your body.

15. KEEP A DAILY JOURNAL

A journal will be your own private record of everything you eat and drink. Enter the date at the top of each page and write the time beside each item you enter. Don't leave out a thing. You will be surprised how much you actually eat each day.

16. SET A GOAL FOR YOURSELF

Only you can decide if you need to lose 5 pounds or 40. But be realistic. Enter this goal in your journal where no one needs to see it but you.

17. SET A DAILY CALORIE GOAL

If you are really serious about losing weight, I suggest you aim at taking in no more than 1,200 calories per day. (When I decide it's time to drop a few pounds, I usually set my goal at 1,000 calories, but I am very careful that what I eat is well-balanced and healthy.) You can actually eat quite well on 1,200 calories, but you will have to choose wisely. A chicken sandwich from Burger King (which I love) has 690 calories so, as you can see, one of those babies and your calorie count for the day is just about shot. Make a game out of adding up your calories each day. Fruits, vegetables and pastas (watch out for the cream sauces) are all good choices.

Remember that exercise burns calories. But, you've got to get serious about exercising for it to do any good at all. A few leg lifts won't burn off that extra slice of pizza. Be honest with yourself about how many calories you're burning off with your exercise program.

Note: The newest way to keep tabs on the food you eat is by counting fat grams. If you read the nutritional information listed on the foods you buy (and you should!), you will notice that more and more foods have a listing of the fat grams they contain. If you are seriously interested in the foods you eat and how they affect your body, I suggest you start reading everything you can find about the fat content in foods. It is quite interesting and may be the secret to weight control.

18. CLIMB ON THE SCALES JUST ONCE A DAY

Weigh yourself at the beginning of your diet, and enter it in your journal. Then weigh yourself daily. I suggest you do it first thing in the morning, after you go to the bathroom, and without any clothes on, if possible. Enter each day's weight in your journal.

19. DON'T GIVE UP

Weight loss comes in waves. You will probably lose a few pounds at first and then level off for a few days. That is perfectly normal, so don't become discouraged. If you keep at it, you will begin to see your weight drop again.

20. REWARD YOURSELF

Set small rewards for yourself. After you have lost five

pounds, do something special, or buy yourself a small gift. The rewards don't need to be big, but if you buy yourself a treat, be sure it's something you can use after you reach your goal. In other words, this is not the time for new jeans.

As I said before, this is not a one-time, quickie diet plan. It is a life-time plan and should be used every day. If you can begin now, as a teenager, to take control of your body and be wise about what you feed it and how you exercise it, you will live a longer and healthier life than most people my age are living. I send my best wishes and highest hopes as you accept the challenge of this life-time body control plan.

Is pain the real reason?

I want to ask those of you who are fighting a weight problem a few very special questions.

Do you ever find yourself eating because you are lonely, or because you feel depressed? Do you seem to reach for food when things are piling up and you feel overwhelmed? Do you eat to escape something in your life? When you're nervous or angry, do you head for the kitchen?

If any of this describes you, don't feel alone. We all reach for things we think will make us feel a little better, a bit more comforted. (Mine is a good, strong cup of coffee!)

Sometimes we even start believing food will make our problems go away. But it doesn't work, does it? Food won't make our problems go away, any more than drinking or taking drugs will. As soon as the "high" is gone, we are right back where we started. The problems are still there, but now we get to add "guilt" to our list of hurts.

Don't spend the rest of your life trying to handle pain by shoving something into your mouth. It won't help. What will help is finding someone to talk with about the pain or loneliness you feel - a school counselor, a minister, a relative, someone you have confidence in and trust.

You CAN find positive ways to deal with the pain in your life.

The insanity of "brand names" ...

The people who make the things we buy know how much we love to spend money—so they keep making more and more things for us to spend more and more money on. And if they are really sharp, they stick a "brand name" on the things they make and advertise them like crazy so we will be desperate to buy them. It's called "consumerism" and, yes, it keeps the economy lively—but it certainly puts a lot of pressure on us to spend more money than we probably should.

No generation of teens has had to face this insanity of "brand names" the way yours does. And I, frankly, don't know how you deal with it as well as you do. Your parents certainly didn't have all this pressure on them, because hardly anything had a "brand name" attached to it years ago. Oh, there were Levi jeans, but they were about the only kind around anyway. We also had Bass Weejuns and Izod shirts. I still get excited when I see a pair of Bass loafers in a store window—probably because I remember how hard I had to work to buy my first pair.

I don't know what we can do about "consumerism." especially the way it affects teenage girls. There is some talk now about making a law that all kids should wear uniforms to school. They do this in many other countries, you know. On the one hand, it wouldn't do much for your creativity or joy in expressing your own tastes and sense of style. But it WOULD take you off the hot seat about this clothes thing. You wouldn't have to spend much time wondering what to wear each day. And it sure would get us back to basics—the basics of looking at each other for what we are rather than what we have on, and judging each other on the basis of kindness, humor, thoughtfulness, and generosity instead of earrings and sweaters and purses and "outfits."

What about the thousands of girls out there who really can't afford all of the "brand names"? What about their feelings? Do any of us even care anymore? Are we all so wrapped up in ourselves that we never see others who may be hurting?

It seems to me, that our obsession with brand names needs to change. Maybe you will be smarter than others have been. Maybe you will know that you can't prove your worth by sticking a label on your body. Maybe you will realize that the worth of a human being goes far beyond any "brand name," that you can't put a price tag on it.

My generation's eagerness to make a buck is no secret, but I think the pressure we have created for you with all our blasted brands is unforgiveable. Maybe you will all get together and make it different.

You ARE beautiful . . .

I wish I could look into your eyes and tell you that you are beautiful, but I can't. So I've tried to say it with this chapter. I pray that you have found yourself somewhere on these pages and have learned how to love and accept yourself more than ever before.

The goal is not to look THE best—there is no such thing. The goal is to look YOUR best—to weigh what's right for YOU, to dress right for YOU, to be smart about what YOU buy and how you spend YOUR money, and to love YOUR body and accept YOUR flaws. The goal is to look into the mirror and smile, not because you've met all the fashion rules, but because you've made your own rules.

And when you have done these things and are headed out the door to meet life head-on, forget about how you look and get on with what's really important—making your life the best it can be.

Section II

Balance: The magic word in surviving life with other people

What to do with all these people? Have you ever heard the old saying, "Can't live with them, can't live without them?" Well, that's usually how most of us feel about the people who share our lives and our space. We can't imagine life without them, but then, too, there are times we can't stand the thought of having them around for another single second.

As you well know, there are three basic kinds of people in your life:

Adults. This group includes people like parents, teachers, and bosses. We also call them the rule-makers. These are the people who can (and are usually happy to) tell you what to do and how to do it. Adults can get on your nerves.

Friends. These are the people who have a huge influence on your life, as you have on theirs. They see you at your best and at your worst. And, as much as you may love being with them, even friends can get on your nerve.

Boys. (You will notice that I saved the best for last.) Personally, I think your relationships with boys—plural, meaning more than one, hint, hint—must have a separate category all by itself because, well, where else would you put boys? They are certainly not ADULTS, and very few of them would qualify as FRIENDS. Boys can get on your nerves BIG TIME. Anyway, you need a lot of help coping with boys these days and you will find it in Chapters 6 and 7.

Adults, friends, and boys are the people we will be talking about in the next five chapters. They are all extremely important of course, because, if you took away any one of these groups, life could get awfully complicated and very dull.

Got to find a way . . .

Okay, so other people are a big deal in our lives, and figuring out how to get along with them is not always easy to do. But we have to find ways or we'll live very lonely lives.

The bonds that develop between people whenever their lives are connected in some way are called "relationships." These relationships include friend to friend, girlfriend to boyfriend, kid to parent, sister to sister, sister to brother, student to teacher, worker to boss, etc. All of us have many relationships with other people. And some of us even manage to have a few GOOD relationships, but not many of us—because good relationships don't come easy.

The magic word . . .

A good relationship can be described with one magic word—"balance." Remember that word, because you will run across it often in the remainder of this book.

A good relationship is balanced. It is found when people share equally and are fair with each other. It is *not* found when one side always wins and the other always loses, nor when one side always has its own way while the other gives in. When one side wants a balanced relationship and the other side couldn't care less, you can forget it—it will never happen.

Good relationships do not come easy. You can't buy one, scream until you get one, bully your way into one, lie down and be walked on to get one, or take abuse to find one. Starting today, if you pay close attention to the people around you, you will begin to see the relationships that are balanced and the ones that are not. You will be quite amazed at how easy it is to see the difference.

In the next five chapters, you will discover how to

have good relationships. And most of all you will find that you need to make some changes if you are going to have them. Be brave enough to make the changes. Don't settle for less.

Three

Adults

Adults are here to stay . . . You can't survive without them. The problem is—surviving WITH them isn't always a piece of cake.

I divide adults into two types—"parents" and "everyone else." (I figure that parents are in a class by themselves, and we'll get to them in the next chapter.)

I know that some of the biggest pain in your life is caused by adults who have never grown up. These adults have never been brave enough to leave childhood and, because they are still children inside, they have no idea how to love and guide you. They just take their own ignorance, anger, and confusion and dump it in your lap. And sometimes what they dump on you is pretty hard to take, isn't it?

Ask almost anyone and, most likely, she can tell you about an adult in her life who disappointed, embarrassed, or hurt her in a way she has never forgotten. But that very same person could also tell you about another adult who was a great example, an exciting teacher or a wonderful friend. Adults come in "good" and "bad" just like everybody else. You have to figure out how to survive the bad ones and enjoy the good ones. There *are* good ones out there, you just have to find them.

People often ask me, "What's the biggest problem with kids today?" My answer is always the same: "They're just trying to figure out how to survive in this world we adults have created."

Adults have always been the ones in charge . . .

Most adults are very quick to find fault with teens. It has always been that way. Plato, who lived over 2,000 years ago and is considered to be one of the wisest men who ever drew a breath, once said, "The young are going to wreck and ruin." A lot he knew. Somehow the human race has continued to survive IN SPITE of all the young people who have lived since Plato graced the planet.

When you stop and think about it, most of the hurtful things that can affect teenagers' lives and can affect what kind of persons they become are *not* problems they themselves create. Divorce, poor education, drugs, violence, poverty, bad family life, physical or sexual abuse, emotional abuse, leaders who don't lead, teachers who don't teach, and families who don't love are problems that happen to young people at the hands of adults. Through no fault of their own, young people can feel their lives affected by such problems, in one way or another.

How soon they forget . . .

Like it or not, if we live long enough, "adult" is where all of us end up—assuming the folks who've made it there before us cut us enough slack so we can manage to do that. You already know that I was a teen in the '60s. What a bunch of loud mouths we were. But guess what we "far-outs" are today? We are ADULTS. We're OLD! We have become the parents, teachers, plumbers, lawyers, nurses, waitresses, bank tellers, ministers, airline pilots, secretaries, carpenters, accountants, and elected officials who run things now. And a lot of us can't shut up about how bad kids are today. Puh-leeze. As if we have room to talk.

Why do the old always fuss about the young? What happens to our memories when we become adults? Do we just forget the way we were, or do we not want to remember? Well, adults should remember more and complain less.

As a matter of fact, I think one of the biggest problems most adults have is a disease called "no memory." And I'm not talking about Alzheimer's.

Do you remember the movie *Back to the Future,* when Marty flipped back in time and met his mom when she was still a teenage girl? She was anything but what he expected. She flirted shamelessly and smoked cigarettes—a regular wild child. Poor Marty was in shock—as we might all be if we could get a peek at what our parents were actually like during their teens. I'm certainly glad my daughters weren't there to see some of my moves.

Every adult living today was a teenager at one time. I know it sounds incredible, but it's true! Most of them have just forgotten about those years, that's all. They have forgotten all the tricks THEY pulled and all the fun THEY had. They have forgotten the pain, curiosity, and joy of being young. Some adults seem to have forgotten everything.

Those little ol' rule makers . . .

By this time in your life you already know many adults. (Maybe a few more than you want to know?) And I know your favorite adults are the ones who make the RULES you must live with. We call those rule-making adults AUTHORITY FIGURES. It makes you cringe, doesn't it?

There is something in all of us that rebels against someone else telling us what to do. We don't seem to mind it so much when we're little. But now that you've hit your teen years, CHANGES happen and I'll bet you've suddenly started wanting to make your own rules. It's not that you are trying to be some smart-mouthed, know-it-all, little jerk face, either. It's simply that you have reached a point in your life where you want to do things your own way.

If that's how you feel, then good for you! That's one of the first signs that you are on the road called "Change." Unfortunately, if you are to travel this road successfully and become the person you want to be, you will have to learn to face the authority figures in your life. And the sooner you face them, the better off you'll be.

What ever happened to "Father Knows Best"?

I know it's very popular these days to make authority figures look like fools. Remember the principal in "Ferris Bueller's Day Off?" And how about those parents in "The Simpsons"? Just like you, I watch the movies and TV shows that make cops seem worse than criminals, parents total dimwits, and teachers worse than stupid. Today's hero seems to be the person who breaks all of the rules and goes against authority.

Believe me, I know many of our authority figures don't deserve all that much respect. I know we have mayors and congressmen and priests and teachers who are real bozos. But for every one of them who lets the rest of us down, there are thousands of others we can listen to and admire.

Maybe those messages telling you to thumb your nose at the rule-makers have gotten through to you, and maybe you are one of those teens who figure you don't have to obey any rules, but I hope not. Because the truth is you'll have a tough time traveling this road called "change" if that's how you feel.

There ARE bosses, parents, and teachers who make rules for us. We must accept this if we are ever to make anything of ourselves and our lives.

What gives them the right!?

I think the easiest way for you to learn how to deal with the rule makers in your life is to first try to understand what gives them the right to be in authority over you in the first place.

This is really pretty simple. People who are in authority over us provide us with something we either need or want. And the more we need what they have or take what they offer, the more authority they will have over our lives.

Look at all the rules we live by that have been made by our government. It has a huge amount of authority in our lives. But, at the same time, look at how much we *have* because of our government. In fact, think of any authority figure you can name and see if this doesn't hold true. Bosses provide us with jobs and money, teachers give us education and a future, parents usually give us everything we need while we're young, and policemen represent the laws we have all agreed to live by and protect us from those who choose not to obey those laws.

I'll try to put it another way. Let's say I have no telephones in my home. (I can't even stand the thought.) If I don't own a phone, the telephone company has no authority in my life—no reason to send me bills—and I have no reason to concern myself with its rules and regulations.

But once I choose to have a telephone in my home, the telephone company begins to have some authority in my life. You can bet it will send me bills, charge me for extra services like "call-waiting," and can even take away my service if I don't keep up my end of the bargain.

Remember what I said about relationships? In a good one, both sides do their best to keep things BALANCED. The phone company gives me good service, and I pay my bill and don't abuse its rules. Whenever you take something from someone, no matter how small it may be, that person will have some authority in your life. Right now, you don't have much choice about the authority figures in your life, but someday you will. Be very careful who you take from because nothing in life is free.

Even with adults, the magic word is "balance" . . .

It's one thing to understand what gives adults the right to be our rule makers, but it's quite another to learn to live with it. When you are young and working so hard to become your own person, it can be awfully hard to live around the people who have authority over you, especially during those times when it seems they are on your back constantly about something. Most of us are trying desperately hard to hang on to our self-respect. Because when we lose that, we've lost ourselves.

Sometimes people who have authority over us seem to take away our self-respect. Maybe they do it without realizing or maybe they have mean hearts and set out to hurt us. However the authority figures in your life behave themselves, I have a suggestion for how you can handle them without losing your self-respect. I believe that if you use this little trick, you will be able to respond to them in a positive way and still feel very good about yourself:

When faced with a rule maker, simply ask yourself two questions:

1. Am I being offered something I need or want?
2. Do I owe something in return?

Let's say the drama teacher has given you a lead part in the school play, but she is one tough cookie to work for. She demands perfect attendance at all rehearsals, that you come to class with all lines memorized, and that there be no joking around or casual conversation during rehearsals. Many of us would look at that kind of authority and say, "Forget it. I'm not going to deal with this woman. She's too hard on me."

But wait, let's go back and ask ourselves the two questions I've suggested.

Am I being offered something I need or want? The answer is "yes." You DO want the part in the play. It's fun and exciting, not to mention that Brigham, the male lead, is gorgeous and you get to kiss him in the third act.

How about question number two?

Do I owe something in return? Again, the answer is "yes." You should say to yourself, "If the teacher respects my work enough to trust me with the lead, I owe her everything I can give to this play. She shouldn't have to tell me to memorize my lines. I should already know them by the time I come to rehearsals. I know we are on a tight schedule and there isn't time for a bunch of goofing off. If I'm serious about being in the play, I should show it."

This is the BALANCE we've been talking about. The teacher gives, so you give. Maybe you are not giving the same things, but you are both giving. That's what makes a good relationship—and a great school play.

They're not supposed to be our pals . . .

While we're on the subject, let's talk about teachers—big-time authority figures. Teachers offer you something you may not especially want sometimes but desperately need—education. Teachers are more important to us than we can imagine. Without them, most of us would be left behind in a world that is fast getting smarter every day.

But somewhere along the way, we might have been misled about our relationship with teachers. We have gotten the idea that we are supposed to LIKE them and that they are supposed to be our FRIENDS. Well, that isn't why teachers go to college. Their job is to teach us, not to be our little buddies. Their part of the deal is to share their knowledge with us, and our part is to LEARN SOMETHING from them. And if all goes as it should, we'll become wiser and much happier people, instead of dimwits. Falling in love with each other is not part of the plan. Teachers teach and we learn. That's the balance. If they don't teach or we don't learn, the relationship is a big flop and we have BOTH wasted each other's time.

If along the way you find a teacher or two you absolutely adore and who make learning the most exciting thing in the world, consider it a real treat. It probably won't happen very often. Be sure to let them know they are very special to you and that you will never forget them, but don't tune out all the other teachers who have wonderful and wise bits of knowledge to give to you just because they don't happen to melt your butter. Learn from them. Take from them the things you can use to better your life. And, in return, give them a terrific student.

How I loved Miss Tapp and Mrs. Emmott and Miss Taylor and Mrs. Ewing. And Frank and Jeanine Teltchik completely changed my life as they shared with me their knowledge of the piano. But, guess what? Some of the teachers I couldn't STAND taught me things I use every day of my life. They gave me knowledge I couldn't live without today. Thinking back, I wish I had given them more in return.

Always there . . .

Authority figures and rules never go away—and I mean NEVER. Even when you are as old as dirt, there will be someone around to tell you what to do. I always thought that by the time I got to the age I am now, I could at least comfort myself by knowing that I would no longer have to answer to anyone but myself. Was I wrong! I answer to rules and regulations all the time. I must admit, though, there is one major difference here: I don't have to answer to my parents like I did when I was your age. (It is a constant source of joy to me that I will never be "grounded" again!)

I guess my least favorite rule makers are those people at the airlines. Not that I have anything personal against them. After all, my husband is an airline pilot, so I understand where they are coming from. It's just that some of their RULES bug me. From the minute you get to the airport, it's one thing after another. You have to stand in line to do EVERYTHING. They ASSIGN you a seat—just like in first grade. They tell you when to get on the plane, where to put your luggage, where to put your purse, when you can eat, when you can drink, when you can go to the bathroom, and then they SUGGEST you wear your seatbelt when seated—they're afraid you might hit the ceiling of the plane if they go through any turbulent air. They also don't want you to gather up your belongings before the plane has landed. (Why wait 'til the last minute?) I've also noticed that they never ask for my opinion about the way they do things. They seem to have the attitude that if I don't like their rules I can just stay on the ground.

Well, since I have to fly often, I keep my opinions to myself. I figure the airlines are providing me with something I both need and want, so I obey their rules and we get along very nicely. I could make a perfect fool of myself by complaining and threatening not to do the things they ask of me, but I figure they know a whole lot more than I do about how to get me safely from point A to point B. So as long as I am riding on their airplanes, I let them be the rule makers in my life. But the minute I'm off that plane, I'm in charge again—that is, until I get to "Baggage Claim" ... then here we go again.

Rules are everywhere ...

Rules, rules, and more rules. They're everywhere—at school, at home, at the mall, at the movies, on the beach, on the highway, in the car—everywhere you look. Sometimes it seems like that's all there is to life. It's probably one of the big reasons why most teens can't wait to grow up and get away from home. "No more rules," they think. HA!

When you're grown, you'll have so many people yammering at you about rules that life back at home will seem like an endless Friday-night slumber party. Once you're out on your own in the big, cruel world, you'll get to face the rules of EVERYONE IN THE UNIVERSE—the college, the dorm, your professors, your sorority, the apartment complex, the light company, the gas company, the water company, the phone company. . . . And don't forget the city, county, state, and federal government rule makers!

Do you know why we have to have so many rules? Because people have a funny way of not always doing what they're supposed to do in life.

If no one ever drove like a fool, there would be no need for traffic laws or motorcycle policemen who hide in the bushes. If no one ever skipped school, there would be no need for rules about attendance or notes from parents. If no one ever took anything that didn't belong to them, we wouldn't have to have burglar bars on windows or locks or security guards. If we all treated each other with love and respect, we wouldn't need courts or lawyers or jails. If we all behaved differently, maybe we wouldn't be surrounded by so many rules. Wouldn't that be wonderful?

"No one can tell ME what to do . . ."

So many of the losers you'll meet in life are simply people who have never learned how to accept any authority in their lives. They are people who thought they were too smart to be told anything—people who refuse to accept any rules. You've seen them.

There is the guy who says, "I'm sick of teachers telling me what to do. I don't have to put up with this anymore." So, he hardly ever shows up for class, refuses to do homework and finally, drops out of school. He has no education, no job—and no future. He really showed those teachers, didn't' he?

Or there is the girl who says, "I'm tired of my parents telling me what to do. They're too strict, and I'm not going to let them run my life any longer." So she runs away from home, ends up on the streets, goes from one guy to another, and, before long, she's on drugs. She has to have money to buy those drugs. And what's the quickest way for a girl on the streets to get money? She becomes a prostitute. And, these days, drugs and prostitution together usually equal AIDS.

It's not just teens who have trouble facing rules. A lot of adults have never learned this lesson, either. These are the same adults we talked about at the beginning of this chapter who bring so much pain into the lives of those around them. These are the ones who can't hold a job, who never finish anything they start, who don't take care of their families, who blame everyone else in the world for their problems, who can't stay away from booze or drugs, who jump from one love affair to another, who are in and out of trouble and sometimes end up in prison.

Well, anyone who lives successfully has already

learned that life has it's rules. And playing by the rules is not a sign of weakness, it's the greatest strength there is.

Grades are 92% attitude . . .

One way to tell how well you're dealing with the rule makers in your life is by looking at your grades. Don't panic—I'm not about to do a 30-page essay on good grades. In fact, I think we put too much importance on grades and not enough on LEARNING.

Grades, of course, are the way we usually measure how much we've learned in school. And, as you well know, kids are greatly judged by the grades they make. It's too bad the teachers aren't.

Grades can make or break us, can't they? Bad ones can ruin a fun year. You can forget sports and school plays and all those other fun extra-curricular activities that make school more tolerable.

But, most important, grades CLASSIFY you. They can put you in the group that's smart and going places or the one that's headed nowhere. I think all of this is a little bit sad, because grades usually have very little to do with intelligence. But they do have a whole lot to do with WILLINGNESS—willingness to work and to do what rule makers ask.

I've noticed that the kids with the good grades are usually the same kids who read, do their homework, get their assignments in on time, and do pretty much whatever else the teachers ask of them. You will find very few scholarship winners hanging around the video arcade. Making good grades pretty well boils down to the desire to do so.

If you have the spirit it takes to make good grades, you will also have the kind of spirit it takes to accomplish any goal that you set for yourself in life. I believe that if you are reading this book, you probably have that kind of spirit I'm talking about. Because I'm talking to the girl who wants the BEST from life—who believes she can make good choices and who wants to make CHANGES in this world.

Do grades really matter? Are they worth the effort? Yes, because when you have paid the price to make good grades, you feel better about yourself and you gain more knowledge—which you can always use. You're labeled a winner, which you are. You're recognized as a leader, which helps you reach other goals. You become eligible for scholarships, which will make college more attainable. And, let's not forget, you'll get one of those great bumper stickers for your parent's car that say, "My daughter is the smartest kid at Puttsville High." Hey, even the bumper sticker alone is worth the effort!

Rule makers can be wrong sometimes . . .

One beautiful Friday afternoon not long ago, I was driving to Palacious, Texas, to speak at the high school. I had one of my "shoo-bop-de-bop" golden oldies tapes blaring and all was well with the world, or so I thought. The speed limit was 65 miles per hour and, since I have a teeny-tiny tendency to speed, I had my cruise control right on 65.

Suddenly I realized there was a Texas Highway Patrolman driving directly behind me. In fact, he was practically in my back seat! He turned on his flashing lights to tell me he wanted me to pull over and stop. I wasn't too happy, but I figured I'd better do what he wanted.

Me (sweetly): "Is there a problem, Officer?"

The Patrolman (his eyes were hidden behind dark glasses): "I clocked you going 61 miles per hour. This is a 65 mile speed zone. You were impeding the traffic."

Yikes! He was telling me that I was driving too slow!

So slowly that I was keeping the traffic from flowing at a normal speed—and he wasn't even smiling! If I hadn't been so mad, I would have died laughing. Me? Driving slowly? Holding up traffic? That'd be the day.

Me (incredulous): "This is impossible. My cruise control was set on 65 and, anyway, how in the world can you IMPEDE anything short of a jet plane if you are moving 61 miles an hour? That's not exactly crawling, you know. And, besides that, there isn't any traffic around here to impede."

Nothing I said made any difference. He had the authority to give me a ticket, and did just that. But this is America, and I have the authority to fight back if I so choose—and I did!

Six weeks later we went to court. The District Attorney was there to represent the Officer, who was still wearing those ridiculous dark glasses, and I represented myself. When it was my turn to tell the jury my story, I mentioned *you*. I said:

"I travel all over the United States talking to teenage girls about taking control of their lives. I speak often to them about answering to the rule makers in our lives. One of the hardest things to explain to a young person is that sometimes we must stand up to authority figures who are unfair.

"This officer has accused me unfairly. I did nothing wrong. I broke no laws. And I am asking you to find me 'not guilty.'

"But whatever the outcome of this case, I want you to know that I will tell this story to teenage girls by the thousands. And I will say to them 'Sometimes authority figures can be wrong. And when they are, be brave enough to stand up for what you believe is right.' "

The jury found me "not guilty."

Listen, if what you are asked to do ever seems truly wrong to you, if a voice deep inside of you says, "This is not right," if you can't get away from the feeling that something doesn't quite add up, . . . then BE BRAVE ENOUGH TO TAKE ACTION. Talk. Scream. Yell. Fight. Do whatever it takes to stand up for what you believe is right. Don't be afraid to listen to your heart.

Someday it will be your turn . . .

Guess who's going to be among the "adults" of tomorrow? You are.

Do you not like how the adults are running things today? Then, make some changes.

Do you feel like most adults don't give a flip about the needs of teens? Then become an adult who knows young people are important.

Do you meet a lot of adults who seem to have been *born* 47 years old? Then become an adult who remembers what it's like to be young.

Do you not know many teachers who act as if they care? Then become a teacher who does care.

Have you been hurt by a boss who was impatient and rude because you didn't work fast enough or learn quickly enough? Then become a kinder boss when you are in charge someday.

Have you been treated like you're just a kid and kids don't really matter? Then decide today that, as long as you live, you will never, EVER treat a young person that way.

You CAN make changes.

You CAN make the world a better place.

Four

Parents

Life with parents can be anything from heavenly to horrifying. If they are terrible, you have to live with it; and if they are wonderful, you got lucky. Some girls adore their parents, and some girls can't stand to be in the same room with theirs. But all girls soon realize that they have no control whatsoever over who or what their parents are.

I have no idea what kind of parents you have. Maybe yours work hard, love and support you, and are pretty cool to be around. Or maybe you have the kind of parents who are abusive, neglectful, and couldn't care less about you.

No matter what they are like, I'll bet you wouldn't mind changing them a bit here and there. Well, sorry, but this chapter won't tell you how to do that—because it's not about changing your parents. It's about helping you to cope, to understand, to learn ways to solve problems, and, most of all, to take responsibility for the kind of person you are.

What is a parent?

Before we go any further, we should first define "parent." (You've been trying to do that for years, right?) As you already know too well, it takes both a male and a female to create a child (and there's far too much of this creating going on, but that's another chapter). Anyway, creating a child is not "parenting." Giving birth to a baby doesn't make you a "mommy" any more than planting a little sperm somewhere makes a boy a "daddy." There is a lot more to parenting than the sexual act that gets the whole thing started.

Now it's wonderful when the two little culprits who did get the whole thing started stick around to lovingly rear this child they've created, but, unfortunately, it doesn't always work out that way—especially these days. Therefore, we can't define "parents" as mommy and daddy.

Sometimes mommy and daddy are nowhere to be found. In fact, the last estimate I've been able to find says that only 7 out of every 100 American families fit all of the following characteristics:

1. one father and one mother who are . . .
2. married to each other and were . . .
3. never married to anyone else and are . . .
4. parenting their own set of children and no others.

So, don't feel like the Lone Ranger if you don't happen to be growing up in a home with your original mom and dad. Neither did I. My parents divorced when I was six, and I was raised by my mother.

Families get wired together in all sorts of ways. Our "parents" can be one single parent, step-parents, grandparents, adopted parents, aunts, uncles, older brothers and sisters, friends of the family, and so on. In spite of all this confusion, I think we can make this "parent" thing real simple.

I say "parents" are those people who provide you with all the things you need to survive—things like shelter, food, and clothing. (You will notice that I did not say provide you with all of the things you want—no one has figured out how to do that yet.) Obviously, someone in your life has been providing these things for you, otherwise you'd be long gone by now. We humans are such helpless little creatures, you know.

So, that's how I define "parents." The people you live with and answer to, the people who provide for you, are your "parents."

It wasn't so bad until the change started . . .

Unless they were horrible meanies (and most parents are not) it was pretty easy to have a good relationship with your parents when you were a baby. In fact, the relationship was extremely "balanced."

Your parents provided you with everything you had—a place to live, bed, food, medicine, toys, shoes, socks. . . . The list could go on for days, but you get the picture.

What did you give them in return? The thing they wanted more than anything else in the world—complete and total control over your life. Let's face it, babies do very little talking back. So, at that time in your life, your parents were 100 percent the boss. They made the rules and you went along for the ride. It was perfect. Everyone was happy.

And then, one day, you began to grow up. The "change" had begun.

Did they change?

When the "change" starts, things have a way of getting real crazy in a hurry. The normal life you've always known goes right out the window and, in its place, trouble walks in. Disagreements soon begin to shake the walls of your once quiet and peaceful home.

You: "I don't want to wear that dress. In fact, I HATE that dress. I want to pick out my own clothes."

Your Parent: "What do you mean, you don't like that dress? I paid good money for that dress, and money doesn't grow on trees, you know."

Or . . .

You: "I don't want to go to Grandma's house Friday night. I'm going to the mall with my friends."

Your Parent: "The whole family is going to Grandma's Friday night and that includes you, young lady. What's the matter with you? You know we always go to Grandma's on Friday."

Or . . .

You: "Can we PLEASE change that radio station? That music is too weird."

Your Parent: "This is MY car and MY radio. You can listen to that stuff you call music in your own room—with the door closed!"

You study your parents in complete amazement. "What's happened to them?" you wonder. They used to be so nice, so easy to get along with. It must be some sort of mid-life crisis. They certainly have "changed." . . . Or, have they?

Or was it you?

What has "changed," my sweet, is not your parents—it's you. You are the one who's becoming a different person, for which you can be very thankful. Can you imagine staying a baby for the rest of your life? Of course you can't. You are now moving ahead and getting on with your life—zippity-doo-dah.

Because you are changing, the relationship you have had all this time with your parents is now becoming very different. It is suddenly out of balance because they are still doing what they have always done and you are not. They are still providing you with all of the things you need to survive, but you no longer want to give them control over your life. Now you want to control your choices.

Here, in a nutshell, is one of the major reasons it's so darn tough to be a teenager. Talk about being between a rock and a hard place! You still desperately need your parents. In fact, you can't survive without them. But you also desperately need to begin finding your own way in life. What a spot to be in! Help!

Strangers are easy to love . . .

You probably hardly ever see parent/teen relationships that are balanced and good. Do you know why? It's because most of us put very little effort into this relationship. It's not something we think we need to work at. We figure the relationship we have with our parents will take care of itself, but it never does.

In fact, most of us have this whole thing completely backwards. We put more effort into having a good relationship with the salesclerk at Macy's than into having one with our own parents. Unfortunately, the result is that we often end up feeling closer to the salesclerk at Macy's.

Sure, there are reasons we choose to be nicer to the

salesclerk. She's so nice to us, never demanding, never asking nosey questions, and never nagging about homework, laundry, or getting off the phone. Why, I'll bet you can't remember the last time you had a cross word with a salesclerk at Macy's, right?

Well, guess what? Everyone seems perfect when you barely know them. It's when you get up close to people that all their warts and fangs begin to show. It's no sweat getting along with people you only see on rare occasions. The real challenge in life is to get along with the ones who are in your face all the time—like your parents.

This one is for you . . .

By now you're probably saying, "Yes, but you don't know my parents." No, I don't know them, but I'll just bet they have faults. I would even go so far as to say that they are far from perfect. How would I know that? Because parents are human beings, and human beings have a way of being "flawed." In fact, sometimes parents' flaws are so bad you shouldn't have to live with them. But that is very unusual. Usually, their faults are not that bad—just bad enough to drive you crazy.

I could fill the next 10 pages telling you about all of the flaws my own parents had. And, if I gave them the chance (which I won't), I'll just bet my daughters could go on for days explaining the many things I did wrong.

Sure, parents can be a pain. But, listen, I didn't write this book for parents—there are plenty of books for them out on the market already. I wrote this book for YOU. I wrote it so that you can become a stronger person—a person who knows how to take control of her life and will make CHANGES in this world we live in. You have a responsibility in the relationship you have with your parents, no matter what their faults are.

Remember this forever: You can never control the

behavior of other people. You can only control your own behavior!

How do you bring balance back into the relationship you have with your parents? There is a way. It's not especially easy, and it *will* take some effort on your part, but you can do it! If you follow the four steps on the following pages, you will see balance come back into your lives, yours and your parents'. Most important, though, you will begin to take control of your own behavior. And that's the greatest thing of all.

Step 1: Be honest.

Lies destroy a relationship quicker than anything else. Yet, we lie to our parents all the time and figure it won't really matter. But it does matter! What if your best friend lied to you, but later you found out about it. How would you feel about her? Would you trust her? Would you always wonder if she was telling you the truth "this time"?

We think that we can lie to our parents, time after time, and that they will still continue to think highly of us and have faith in us. Why should they? It takes an extremely strong person to stand up and admit the truth, even when it hurts. And it also takes a strong person to do what your parents ask of you, even when you want to do something else. Not many people have that kind of strength anymore. Most of us want so much to have our own way we don't mind lying to get it. But, in the long run, we only hurt ourselves; we never win when we lie. And even if you are able to fool your parents, you can never fool yourself.

Be honest. It pays off bigtime.

Step 2: Get your work done.

Do you want your parents to stop treating you like a baby? Then don't act like a baby.

Do you want them to trust you with more freedom? Then show them you deserve to be treated like someone who is growing up, someone who can be trusted.

You can do this by meeting your daily responsibilities, whether it's doing homework, washing the dishes, doing laundry, cleaning your room, feeding the cat, practicing the piano, or whatever it is you have to do each day. Don't put it off! Don't even give your parents the chance to mention it to you. Don't make them nag at you. And don't make excuses for why it's not done. Surprise them! Shock them! Shock yourself! Just get in there and do it!

Step 3: Honor your parents.

To show honor means to show outward signs of respect through words AND actions. It means to say old-fashioned things like, "yes ma'am" and "no sir"—not because you are less a person than either of your parents, but because you are too much a person to do otherwise. Showing honor means to listen to what your parents say, to do what they ask, and not to speak to them rudely. Putting down your parents is putting yourself down.

Are you saying your parents don't deserve to be treated with honor? Okay, maybe they don't, but you aren't reading a book called "Parent Power." You are reading "Girl Power." It's *your* life we care about here, not theirs. It's *your* future that is before you. It's *your* self-esteem we want to build. When you honor your parents, you are a very unusual and special teenager—someone the world needs.

Step 4: Show your love.

I've told this story many times, and it's still very precious to me:

When I first began my "Pink Flash" seminars for teenage girls, everyone in my family was well aware of the hard work and long hours I had spent in preparation. It had taken a year's worth of research, reading, and meetings, but—finally—everything was set to go.

A few days before I was to leave town for the very first seminar, I found on my desk a package of pink notebook paper, a small pink calculator, and a pink note that read:

Dear Mom,

Just to show how much I support the things you do, I bought you some "pink" things.

I love you, Hilary

My daughter, who was 14 at the time, had put this little surprise together for me. She had had her older sister take her shopping and, using her own money, she had carefully chosen items she thought I could use. After I wiped the tears from my eyes, I placed that little note inside my "Pink Flash" workbook, and it is still there today. I have carried it with me all over the United States.

Do you show your parents you love them? Are you interested in their lives? Do you show concern for their problems? Do you listen while they talk? Do you ask how their day went? Have you ever written a loving note to them? Do you call just to say hi? Do you hug them? Do you talk to them when you don't really want anything?

If you haven't been doing these things, why not try sometimes? Just see if they don't help make a difference.

Learn from your yesterdays . . .

Ask girls what they dislike most about their parents and most of them will say "their rules." I can relate to that. My Mom had some rules that would choke a goat. But along with being the parent comes the right to lay down the law, so part of the deal is that the parent gets to be the rule maker.

It would be perfectly pointless for me to tell you to try to like your parent's rules, so I won't. That would be like telling you to enjoy your booster shots. But maybe if you could understand the rules a bit better, and where they come from, they might be easier to swallow. And the best way to do that is to look to the past.

When you were three, there was probably a rule at your home not to touch the hot stove. Your parents warned that if you did touch it, you'd get burned. Maybe not being so sure that your parents were quite the authority on heat they thought they were, you decided to find out for yourself. So you touched the stove and burned the bejabbers out of your pudgy little hand. Suddenly the rule made sense.

Now move ahead to when you were five. Sitting in a movie theater, patiently waiting for the movie to begin, just doing what any five-year-old does when bored to death, you began to pick your nose. Your Dad pushed your hand away from your face and told you not to do that anymore. You wondered what his problem was and decided to find another way to pass the time. "What a grouch," you thought. "When I get older, I'm gonna pick my nose all I want."

But several years later, maybe, you found yourself sitting beside your little brother at the movies, and looked over just in time to see the little geek picking his nose. You screamed bloody murder and pointed out to everyone in the theater what a perfectly gross human being you had for a brother. Then you remembered. You used to do the very same thing yourself. And suddenly the rule made sense.

You see, the truth about hot stoves and picking your nose in public didn't change—you did. You changed. You grew up. You began to think differently.

Is it possible that one of these days, because of changes that will happen to you as you grow older, some of the rules your parents have for you today will suddenly begin to make more sense? Is it possible that you'll someday understand the reason for a curfew? Is it possible that you'll someday understand why your parents nag you about studying and improving your grades? Is it possible that you'll begin to understand why they don't want you to run around with a certain group at school? Is it possible that sooner or later you'll understand why they give you jobs to do and responsibilities to meet? Are all these things just a little bit possible?

I know some of their rules may NEVER make any sense to you. (Although, it is sort of strange the way most teens grow up and set the very same set of rules for THEIR kids.) I'm still convinced that a few of my mother's rules came straight from "The Twilight Zone," but—when I really stop and think about it now—most of those rules made pretty good sense.

What is a good parent?

I've not yet had a girl tell me she wished she had bad parents. In fact, I get more letters from girls like you about problems with their parents than about any other subject. I understand that you truly want to get along with your parents. But I sometimes wonder if you really know what a good parent is.

Having good parents is something you rarely enjoy until you are older, because parents can be a real pain while you are young (especially during your teen years). They make it their business to find out everything that's going on in your life—at least, as much as they possibly can.

Good parents want to know every last detail about that boy you seem to be so interested in. They ask a million questions . . . about your friends, your friends' parents, and even your friends' friends! They give you a curfew—earlier, it seems, than anyone else in the entire universe.

Good parents show up at school functions. They keep tabs on your grades. They ask you about homework. They want to meet your teachers. They make a lot of noise about "a balanced diet."

Good parents have three favorite questions: "Where are you going?" "Who will you be with?" and "When will you be back?" They can recite by heart the amount of sex and violence in any movie made in the past 20 years. They have very interesting opinions about MTV and are happy to share them with all your friends. They love to give you little jobs around the house. And they insist you do something about that room of yours.

Good parents remind you to stand up straight. They ask that you speak to them respectfully and can get pretty stressed out when you don't. They usually say the same thing every time you walk out the door—"Be careful." And they don't seem to care a whole heck of a lot about what everyone else's parents have to say. They listen and are willing to talk. They don't mind taking on the job of being the "adult" in the relationship.

Good parents hug you, even when you think you're too old to be hugged. And they never seem to get tired of saying "I love you." So, do you still think you want good parents? They can be a real pain.

Very real pain . . .

I think it's so interesting the way everyone runs around foaming at the mouth these days about how drugs are ruining the lives of our young people. Don't get me wrong: I definitely think using drugs is a stupid, dangerous cop-out. But I don't think drugs are the biggest problem facing young people today—and neither do most of you.

Most of you think your parents should receive that honor. When I questioned girls like you in my survey about "the biggest problem in your life," 48 percent answered "problems with my family." They listed things like "my parents don't spend time with me," "I never see my dad," "my parents fight all the time," "I can't talk openly and honestly with my parents," "my mom's boyfriend is a total jerk," and "my parents don't seem to care about my feelings."

So many girls like you gave these answers. I could feel the pain as I read their comments on the survey—the pain from feeling unimportant, from feeling sad thoughts like "I don't matter to anyone." Many girls try to numb that pain with drugs, alcohol, too-early sex, or too much food. None of those are the answer to resolving the problems, or the pain.

I know such pain may be very real to you. And I understand that, sometimes, nothing can be done to make the relationship with your parents loving and free. But, before you give up, I want you to try a couple of suggestions I've listed on the next few pages. With a little extra effort on your part, maybe you can get those "talk lines" open between you and your parents. Maybe, because you care, you will be able to bring about some changes in the relationship. It's worth a try.

Idea 1: Sit down and have a talk.

You'll notice that I said "Sit down," and not "While running through the room, scream at your parents over your shoulder that you think there might be a slight problem between you."

Put forth the effort to set a time with your parents to

sit down and talk. Take the responsibility for this yourself. Try saying: "Mom (or Dad), I think we need to talk. When would you have time for us to sit down together?"

Before you begin your talk, you might suggest that everyone have something to drink, like a cup of tea or a cool drink.

Find a quiet place where you won't be disturbed. Turn off the television and turn on the telephone answering machine, if you have one, or have someone else take calls for a while.

It's better if others who aren't involved in the problem aren't present for this talk—this is not a group sport. If the problem is between you and your dad, then you and your dad should be the ones talking. On the other hand, if the problem is between you and your dad but your dad won't talk about it, try involving your mom or someone else who might act as a go-between for you and your dad.

Showing this much interest in solving the problem will impress upon your parents how much you care about your relationship with them.

Idea 2: Talk during the "talk."

You must open your mouth and communicate. Otherwise, how in the world will the problem ever be solved?

A big complaint from your parents might be that when they try to talk with you, you clam up and won't say a word. Explain your side of the story. Don't be afraid to say honestly how you feel.

Think your feelings through ahead of time and if it will help, make a list of the things you want to say. Try not to become frustrated when the conversation doesn't go exactly as you'd like. Just keep trying to communicate your feelings. Speak softly, but firmly. And don't be rude or vulgar—that will only make the problem worse.

Idea 3: Listen.

There is a big difference between talking and arguing. Don't argue. Show that you are mature enough to understand that your parents have feelings too and that you are interested in hearing their side of the story. Be willing to listen to what they have to say.

Go into this conversation knowing that you will need to meet your parents halfway if the problem is to be solved. For instance, if the issue is your curfew and they want you in earlier than you feel is fair, try offering to come in even earlier than they are asking on nights when nothing special is going on. Then, in exchange, ask if they will let you stay out later on nights when you have big plans. Be ready to give a little. Compromise is the name of the game. After all, that's what "balance" is all about.

A good guideline to go by is this: If you find yourself talking more than listening, it's time to zip it for a while and let Mom or Dad have the floor for a change.

Idea 4: Write a letter.

Talking face to face doesn't always work. Sometimes everything comes out wrong and the problem seems worse than when you started. If that's the case, why not write a letter to your parents? Writing is a wonderful way to communicate.

Sit down in a quiet place and put your thoughts on paper. Write those words that are so hard to say when looking your parents straight in the eye. After all, teenage girls write the most beautiful letters in the world.

Give your letter to your parents at a time when it will be a while before you are together again, like in the morning before you leave for school. Then they will have the whole day to think about your words and feelings. That evening, when you are together again, you will both have had time to think clearly about your problems.

Idea 5: Don't give up.

Even when things seem darkest, don't give up. These are your parents and, even though you might not think so, they probably love you more than you can imagine. They will be in your life for a long time and, no matter how far away from home you go, the memory of their faces and the sound of their voices will always be by your side.

Don't ever stop reaching for a good relationship with them. It's worth every effort you make.

Someone else there for you . . .

Okay, so now I've given you some great suggestions about ways to solve problems with parents. But I do understand that there may be times when nothing seems to work. Sometimes the problems are too big—you can't talk without fighting, no one wants to compromise, and the whole thing is impossible.

If this happens, will you please find an ADULT to talk with about your problems? Talking to your best friend may be comforting, but do you really think she has the experience and maturity to give you the advice you need to hear? After all, your friends are probably having the same problems and going through the same things you are right now. You need to talk with someone who has had a little more time to work through those painful lessons of life. You need advice from someone who has been there and come out on the other side.

There is an adult in your life right now who cares about you and the problems you are having. Maybe it's a teacher or a counselor at school. Maybe it's a minister, a priest or a rabbi. Maybe it's an aunt, a grandparent, or a neighbor.

I had an aunt and uncle who never seemed to mind

listening to all of my problems when I was a teen. I felt like I could tell my Aunt Bonnie and Uncle Randy anything and that they would always be there for me. They were more important in my life than they will ever know.

I know there is someone there who cares about you. Look around; when you need them, they will be there.

Sometimes you can only save yourself . . .

So far, now, we've talked about building good relationships with your parents, and about what you can and should do to make that happen. But, in some families, there are times when the parents have such huge problems it's impossible for them to have a good, balanced relationship with their own teenaged kids. Sometimes they are unable to hold up their end of the bargain. If that ever happens in your own family, the most important thing for you to know is that it's not your fault; the problem is with the parent, not with you.

I believe that if all parents were good and loving, we would have few (if any) problem children. But in the real world, not all parents are good and loving. It may be impossible to have a good relationship with a parent who is alcoholic, or drug addicted, or who won't work, or who runs away from responsibilities as a parent. And, in my opinion, a parent like that doesn't deserve your respect—your love, yes, but not your respect.

If you have good parents, please appreciate them. But, if you don't, I hope you will make up your mind to save yourself. Plan for your own future. Decide that you will not let the failure of your parent ruin the rest of your life. Decide that you will not be that kind of parent to your children. Concentrate on your own life and on how you wish to live someday. Maybe, in time, that parent will get better so that your relationship can have a chance to heal. Until then, love that person as best you can, but SAVE YOURSELF.

You can survive a bad parent, and, on the next few pages, I'll tell you how.

Understanding abuse . . .

Abuse is a horrible word, but not nearly as horrible as the actions behind it. Every day, many teenage girls suffer from some sort of abuse—abuse that will affect the rest of their lives—and maybe even the lives of their husbands and children someday.

Usually, abusers are people who are very close to us: family members, neighbors, friends, or even teachers and ministers. They are people we know and want to trust.

That's why abuse is so hard to stop. If a total stranger walked up to you and hit you, everyone would rush to your aid and offer you help, but when your own father hits you, it's a different story. People around you often refuse to see the abuse. They close their eyes to it. They don't want to listen when you try to tell them of the awful thing that has happened to you. And sometimes their unwillingness to help hurts almost as much as the abuse itself.

You will never be able to handle abuse effectively without first knowing exactly what it is—and what it is not. After you have read the next few pages, you will have a very clear picture of what abuse is. And, if you yourself should ever suffer from abuse, you will know how *you* can put a stop to it.

Abuse comes in many forms . . .

Abuse means to treat someone badly. It means to misuse or treat in a hurtful way. You do not value someone you abuse.

Abuse is one of the most terrifying things happening to teenage girls today. And, as you can see in the result of my survey of teenage girls like you, many girls suffer every day because of abusive treatment. There are three basic kinds of abuse that can affect your life as a teenage girl: (1) sexual abuse, (2) physical abuse, and (3) mental or emotional abuse.

If you are suffering from any kind of abuse, it could have a huge influence on the rest of your life and how you value yourself as a person. And if you read anything on the next few pages that sounds painfully familiar to you but aren't sure why, it may be because you have blocked it out of your memory. When horrible things happen to us as children, we often choose not to remember them. No matter what has happened to you in your life, facing it is the first step to putting it behind you. And, for those of you who do need to face this issue of abuse, please know that you are not alone.

Abuse that is sexual . . .

Sexual abuse is a teenage girl's worst nightmare. I believe that sexual abuse does more damage to your mind and future than any other kind of abuse. Sexual abuse, like physical abuse, is an attack on your body, but it is done for sexual reasons—insane reasons only the abuser can know for sure. Sexual abuse can be many different things—from someone touching your body in a way that makes you uncomfortable to rape.

Here are a few guidelines that should help you:

- There should never be any sexual activity between you and another person without your permission.
- No one should ever touch your body in a way that makes you feel nervous or unsafe.
- You should never be forced to touch any part of

another person's body in any way that makes you feel nervous or uncomfortable.

- You should have total control over every area of your body.
- The private areas of your body, such as your breasts, vagina, and buttocks, should never be touched in any way by anyone without your permission. (Sometimes we must be examined by doctors or nurses for health reasons, and these areas of our bodies are included in the exam. This is not sexual abuse.)
- You should not be teased about your "periods" or the development or growth of your body.
- No one should make rude or vulgar remarks to you about sex, about your body, or about their own bodies.
- You should never be forced to sit on someone else's lap.
- There should be no long kisses between you and anyone else (especially an adult) without your permission.
- You should be allowed privacy while you dress and bathe—no one should be there without your permission.

Knowing how to react to sexual abuse is very important:

- If something makes you uncomfortable, you should be able to tell your family how you feel, and your feelings should be respected.
- If you are ever forced to do something concerning your body that you do not want to do, it is WRONG and you have the right to fight back.

Abuse that is physical . . .

Physical abuse is also an attack on your body. It can be very painful both to our minds and to our bodies.

Here is a list of things to help you understand what physical abuse is:

- No one should ever hit you in anger.
- No one should shove you or hold you down.
- No one should ever hit you with an object that would bring great pain to your body, such as a board or a belt buckle. No one should ever cut your body or twist your arms.
- You should never be tied down or locked in a closet.
- You should never be forced to go without food or water for long periods of time.
- You should not be tickled until you cry or scream for help.
- Anything that brings great pain to your body is abuse.

What about spanking? A badly misbehaving child might sometimes need a restrained spanking—to get his attention, but there is a very big difference betweeen spanking a child and beating the tar out of a kid. To beat someone is to physically abuse them, and good parents understand the difference.

I believe that by the time you have become a teen, spanking doesn't make much sense. If you have a behavior problem that your parents feel needs to be corrected, there are much better ways to get your attention—like grounding or restricting you from certain activities, or revoking telephone privileges.

Parents who really care about their children insist that they obey important family rules. That's one of the ways a good parent prepares you to face life. But parents who really care about their children DO NOT abuse them.

Abuse that is emotional . . .

Mental or emotional abuse is the hardest abuse to describe. Perhaps all teenagers at one time or another feel like they are being mentally abused by their parents—I know I certainly did. There is a big difference between having a parent tell you things you don't want to hear and being mentally abused.

Perhaps this will help you understand the difference. Mental abuse is not an attack on the body, it is an attack on the mind. Mental abuse comes to us in words spoken by someone important and powerful in our lives—words that make us feel stupid or ashamed or unloved.

Abusive language is words full of hate and anger, words that can cut as deeply as any knife, words that we carry like heavy baggage for the rest of our lives. Abusive words tell us we are failures and take away our hope and belief in ourselves. They are words that take just a bit more life from us each time they are spoken.

Mentally and emotionally abusive parents are the ones who tell their kids how stupid they are. They are the ones who scream at their kids in front of other people. They make fun of their kids. They never listen. They only talk, talk, talk.

It is not your fault . . .

The first step toward solving any problem is understanding it. I believe that you now understand what abuse is, so, the very next thing I want you to understand is that it is not your fault.

It is very natural for a girl who is being abused to feel that it is her fault, that she has done something to deserve the treatment she has received, but nothing could be further from the truth!

In fact, many abusers will try to convince you of one of the following lies:

1. It is your fault.
2. There is nothing wrong with what they are doing to you.

This is the abuser's way of trying to control you. The abuser knows that if you tell anyone about the abuse you have suffered he or she will be in BIG trouble, so the abuser tries to convince you of these lies in order to keep you quiet.

If any of the abuse discussed in the past few pages is happening to you, the first thing you MUST do is find someone to talk to. And I don't mean tomorrow or next week—I mean right now. Don't wait another minute. There are thousands of people and hundreds of agencies that are there to protect and defend you. In fact, you have the whole United States government on your side! But you must be the one to take action. No one can help you if you do not ask for it. Please, please, do not let any abuse in your life continue. Reach out for help NOW.

One last thought about you and your parents . . .

I don't want to end this chapter on such a horrible subject as abusive parents. Most parents are not abusive. Most parents love their children more than they love their own lives, and the mistakes they make in parenting are from ignorance, not hate. We do hear many stories of abused kids these days, but there are far more kids out there whose names are never in the news, who are loved and cared for every day of their lives by parents who would gladly do anything for them.

Parents, like all adults, come in both "good" and "bad." I hope, after reading this chapter, you know what a good parent is—and what a bad parent is. You may have already admitted to yourself that you have pretty good parents after all.

No matter who your parents are or how they behave

themselves, the most important thing for you to remember is that you can't control them. You can only control yourself. You are not responsible for their failures or successes, but the failure or success of your own life is up to you.

Before we leave the subject of parents, I want you to ask yourself one question. Answer it honestly, for it may help you, more than anything I've said so far, to look closely at the role you play in the relationship with your parents. Ask yourself: If I were a parent today, would I want *me* for a daughter?

Five

Friends

When you really stop and think about it, friends are like your own personal "Declaration of Independence" because they're usually one of the first things you get to choose and have all by yourself. We don't ask our parents' opinion before we choose a friend. And because we generally find that we would rather be with our friends than with anyone else, choosing friends becomes like a first giant step away from home and family, choices we make all alone And finding a new friend is one of life's little miracles.

A friend is someone you truly enjoy being with—a person who likes the things you like and, at least part of the time, thinks the way you think. A friend is someone you share your most secret thoughts with—someone you know you can trust. A friend makes you feel comfortable.

Friends are those people in your life who see you close up, who know you well, and who like you anyway. And the friends you choose let everyone know the kind of person you are becoming, because who they are says a lot about YOU—what you value, what you believe in, and, in many ways, what you think of yourself.

Best friends are few and far between . . .

Thousands of books have been written about friendship. It's a word we toss around a lot. But for all the books and all the talk, true friendship is not something you will find very often on this planet.

I always worry a bit about the girls who claim to have lots and lots of "best" friends. Best friends just don't come that easily in life. First of all, "best friendships" don't happen instantly, and they are not something you should ever take for granted. But once you've found a best friend, she never really leaves you. You may move away from each other or grow into different people who can't share a future the way you have shared the past, and you may not see each other for long periods of time. But somehow those things don't seem to matter so much because best friends—true best friends—always carry a part of each other deep in their heart, where only a select few are ever invited and only a select few are brave enough to go.

Having tons of best friends isn't really the point, anyway. It's having a few good, dear friends that counts. And if you have that, you will be way ahead of most people.

How will you find these few dear friends? Well, you'll probably find them when you aren't really looking (the same way you bump into the best guys). You'll be out there in life, happily doing your own thing, when, suddenly, you will realize that you have discovered a special human being. And that may be the beginning of a beautiful friendship. Time will tell. Beautiful friendships happen because of . . . but you already know the answer to that one. It's called "balance."

An old idea . . .

Here is where the "balance" in relationships starts to get interesting. Up until now, the balance we've talked about has been this sort of painful thing you almost have to force yourself to do . . . Remember what we said earlier: "If you are going to have a good relationship with your parents or your teachers, you have to do your part to keep things balanced." I mean, the thought is great—it's what we should all do—but that doesn't necessarily make it fun.

On the other hand, building a balanced relationship with a friend *is* fun, and it pays off big-time on the weekends.

When I was a little girl, my mother taught me something called The Golden Rule: "Do unto others as you would have them do unto you." The words didn't mean much to me when I was five. They sounded like another silly nursery rhyme, but I said them often, usually at Mother's suggestion. "Do unto others, blah, blah, blah . . . "

As I grew older, the words seemed to change or . . . maybe I began to change. The words began to make a lot of sense to me. I should treat people the way I want them to treat me—simple as that. That's really what all this friendship stuff is about. The balance is found in being to others what I would like for them to be to me: kind, honest, fair, trustworthy, and understanding. Isn't this a neat idea? You'd never dream that the idea has been around for thousands of years, would you?

Forget "peer pressure" . . .

I've heard enough about "peer pressure" to last me a lifetime. And I'll bet you have, too. I don't believe in peer pressure. At least, not the way everyone talks about it.

The dictionary tells us that a "peer" is someone of

equal standing. Your peers are those people who are like you, and mine are like me—same age, lifestyle, interests, fears and hopes. My peers are not 16 years old—not if I am mentally healthy, that is. My peers have outgrown the zit stage, don't get much out of a slumber party anymore and talk a lot about things like taxes and house payments. Your peers probably still live at home with their parents, go to school every day, like their music loud, and are making big plans for the future.

Now, it is very natural and normal to be INFLUENCED by the choices of our peers. If we see our peers wearing a certain style of clothing, we decide we want to wear the same thing. If we notice our peers speaking or acting in a certain way, we may consider mimicking their actions. Everyone does this, not just teenagers.

In fact, adults are a thousand times worse than teens when it comes to being suckers for peer influence. Why do you think so many adults have their credit cards maxed out and are in debt up to their eyeballs? It's so they can drive the "hottest" cars to the "trendiest" restaurants while wearing the "latest" fashions. They build their entire lives around what's "hot" and what's "not!"

Peer INFLUENCE is very real. But, peer PRESSURE? Nah. You feel plenty of pressure in life, all right, but very little of it is coming from your friends. Most of it is coming from people who want your *money*.

Friends are not the real culprits . . .

If I asked you to name the problems teens face that are most often blamed on peer pressure, you'd probably come up with the same list I've made and it would range from the pressure to buy brand names to drugs, alcohol and sex. But are these problems really created by your "peers"?

Have you ever seen a pair of tennis shoes that you

honestly felt were worth $150? Am I the only person on Earth who finds the price tags on those horrible looking things incredible? Show me a pair of tennis shoes worth that much money and I'll actually put them on my feet. Those awful shoes are designed, manufactured, advertised, and sold by adults who work very hard to make their products look attractive to the rest of us. Many parents will scream that they just HAD to buy those shoes for little Susie because she was under such "peer pressure" to have them. That's a bunch of baloney. Little Susie may be INFLUENCED because she sees all of the other kids wearing these shoes; but the pressure she feels, just like the pressure her little pals feel, comes from experts who know how to bend kids' brains.

The results of some of this pressure can be much more serious—the pressure in our society to use alcohol, for instance. Alcohol is a drug, by the way, and it's the one most often used by teens these days. Why do you think most teens drink? Because it seems like the "adult" ticket to fun and good times. And why would teens think that? Because beer commercials are the greatest commercials on TV and do a tremendous job of convincing us that the way to party, bond with friends, and have fabulous times is by drinking. Who makes those commercials? Teens? Not quite.

Adults make them. (Adults, by the way, who make lots of money.) They have convinced millions of us that fun is found in a six-pack. But the unfortunate truth is, alcohol's a killer. It can kill people, or the people who use it sometimes kill people, or cripple them for life, when they climb behind the wheel. Or maybe they just make poor choices they never would have made when sober, all in the name of "fun." Isn't it unbelievable that we say "Just Say No" to drugs and then advertise on prime-time television the very drug that kills and cripples thousands more every day than all other drugs put together?

Remember when you were little and the best commercials were the ones advertising cereal? This very same kind of pressure was being put on you then, only it was aimed at little folks. After you had spent just one Saturday morning watching cartoons (and in the process had also viewed about 400 cereal commercials), you drove your mom nuts begging for that cereal you HAD TO HAVE.

As you grow older, cereal loses its thrill. More adult products start to catch your eye, and you begin to pay closer attention to the advertising for those products. An ad showing a bunch of gorgeous people who are all drinking the same brand of beer and playing volleyball at the beach looks very attractive to you. THIS is where the pressure starts. People who advertise and sell products know what they're doing and know how to make us want their products. You never hear the truth about drinking in those commercials. You never hear about the broken homes and shattered lives due to alcoholism. You never hear about how many teens lose their lives every year due to drunk driving—a big percentage of them dying on prom night.

Commercials and advertising will always be with us, but we can be smarter about the way we respond to the pressure coming from those ads. We don't have to believe everything they say. We don't have to let them do our thinking for us. We don't have to buy their products.

It can go either way . . .

The fact that I pooh-pooh peer pressure doesn't change my strong feelings about peer influence. The influence we have on our friends, and they have on us, is unbelievable. And it can go either way. Sometimes it's the greatest thing that can happen and sometimes it's the worst. It depends on the friend, and on you.

I knew a girl once (we'll call her Amy) whose attitude about school wasn't exactly what you'd call inspiring. Her grades were below average and she just sort of slid by. Then one day she started liking a boy (you know how quick these romances can start) who was in honors classes and very involved in school activities. His can-do feelings about school showed in his commitment to homework and willingness to do extra assignments. As Amy and this boy began to date, she also started hanging around many of his friends, who were straight-A students themselves. Before long, Amy was making straight As, too, because her new friends helped change her attitude about school. (I say "helped" because no one can "change" you but yourself.)

You see, I don't buy this picture of some poor little girl who goes out, suddenly gets involved with the wrong crowd and, whoops, two minutes later, she's on drugs and headed for a life of crime. I don't think it's quite that simple. If a girl gets involved with the wrong crowd, there's a reason she made that choice. Maybe she was looking for excitement because she thought hers was the most boring family in the world. Maybe she was looking for acceptance because no one seemed to love her exactly as she was. Maybe it was anger. Maybe curiosity. Whatever the reason, SHE made the choice.

I think Amy probably made the choice to like that certain boy because she saw in him things she wanted to be. When it comes to friends, we all make our own choices—choices that can affect the rest of our lives.

The choice is always yours . . .

The reason I'm making such a big deal about distinguishing between "peer pressure" and "peer influence" is this: When you've finished reading this book, I want you to believe one thing with all your heart—YOU can control your destiny. And the only way you will believe that is if you know about your choices. In all of the relationships you have with other people—adults, parents, friends, boys—YOU have choices to make. Even though you're young, you don't have to be a victim of other people's actions. You may be "influenced" by others, but you don't have to be "pressured" into doing things you don't want to do.

No one can control your life but you—friends can't, boys can't, and adults or parents who would choose to harm you can't. When you understand this and live by it, changes will come. But there's still a long way to go, and there's a lot more work to do, so read on.

In the next few pages, you'll find what it takes to be a good friend and a good influence. As you read, grade yourself on the kind of friend you are, and then grade the way your friends influence you. You'll probably feel very differently about your influence on your friends, and theirs on you, by the time you've finished reading this chapter.

Loyalty

If there is one thing missing from most friendships today, it's loyalty. In fact, it almost seems as if we don't have use for this word anymore. Loyalty means being constant and faithful. True friendship always has a kind of faithfulness to it, a way of staying true blue even in the tough times.

A loyal friend will not talk about you in a negative way behind your back. A loyal friend doesn't make fun of you to others. A loyal friend is the first to name your good points and the last to remember your bad ones. All of us wish for loyal friends, but few of us are strong enough to become one.

Acceptance

True friends accept each other for what they are. They don't set about to change each other—no matter how much they may wish they could. Not that this acceptance is blind, mind you. It's perfectly normal to see the difference between yourself and your friends. After all, if there were no differences, you and your friends would be bored to death.

True friends welcome their differences and think it's okay to see things from other viewpoints. Accepting someone means to let them fly, and feel, and think, and do. You cannot have a truly good friendship without acceptance.

Honesty

Lies always kill, and good friends know this. They know a lie will ruin their friendship quicker than anything else. And once trust is gone, very little can take its place.

Being honest is not always the easy thing to do, nor the most pleasant. Often, it requires time and tears. But a good friend does not back away from the truth. And the best friends of all are the ones who are willing to tell you the truth even when you don't want to hear it.

Equality

This characteristic brings us back to the basic idea of balance. A good friend would never expect things to be done her way all of the time. Good friends share. Good friends give one another choices. Good friends listen to each other's opinion. Good friends take turns doing everything, no matter how large or how small.

You will probably have to remind yourself from time to time to maintain this equality, this balance, because it's human nature to rock along doing things *our* way until someone screams that it's their turn. But fairness and equality are always there when you find truly good friends.

Thoughtfulness

This is my favorite characteristic of a good friend. "Marked by careful thinking. Considerate of others." That's how the dictionary defines "thoughtful." Wouldn't you love to have a friend who "carefully thinks" about you? So much pain is caused by people who don't think or consider or care about the feelings of others.

A thoughtful friend remembers your birthday, tells you when your slip is showing, and notices when your hair looks great. A thoughtful friend sends a silly card for no reason and is never too busy to listen. A thoughtful friend laughs with you and cries with you and doesn't mind doing either one. If I could have a wish for you, it would be that life would bring you at least one thoughtful friend.

A game with an eye opening message . . .

I grew up believing that teenage girls gossiped more than anyone else in the world. Then I married an airline pilot and decided that pilots gossip more than anyone—I think it's all that time they spend cooped up in airplanes. Anyway, girls and women do love to talk, don't they? We especially like to talk on the phone.

Talking is very important. It helps us learn about ourselves. Talking lets our thoughts and feelings out into the open where we can see them, hear them, and look at them more closely. A friend of mine says, "If I can hear it, I can heal it." Yes, talk can be very healing—or it can be a killer, especially when the talk becomes "gossip."

Gossip is hateful, hurtful talk that can ruin a person's life. Most people who gossip never intend to bring pain and suffering into the lives of those they talk about. They've just heard a juicy story, that's all, and can't wait to share it with someone else. But that's the problem. Every time a story is retold, it takes on new life and soon grows into a breathing, living monster.

Whenever I get the chance, I love to use this game as a way of showing girls just like you how easy it is for all of us to say things about other people that may not be true. The next time you've got a gang of girls together, try it. The object is to tell a story and then see how different it becomes each time it is repeated.

Here's how it works: Get a group of at least 10 or 12 girls together. Have half of them leave the room. Write out a story that's not too hard to remember. Here is an example:

> "Courtney and Kyle had an argument in P.E. class. As Courtney was walking to her next class, she saw Russell coming out of principal's office. Courtney stopped to tell Russell about her argument with Kyle. They both looked up and saw Mr. Richardson, the principal, coming down the hall. Courtney and Russell hurried off to class so they wouldn't be tardy."

Have ONE of the girls who left the room return, and read the story to her. (This is so there will be no doubt that the story started off correctly.) Then have a second girl return. Have girl Number 1 tell the story (by memory) to girl Number 2. Then have a third girl return to the room. Have girl Number 2 tell the story to girl Number 3.

Continue to bring the girls in one at a time until all have returned. Each girl will be told the story by the girl who came back into the room just before her. Finally, the last girl reentering the room gets to tell the story to everyone.

You'll be amazed how much the story will change. By

the time the last girl tells it, it won't even sound like the story you first read. This is a good example of how easy it is to spread a lie.

I'll never forget Wanda . . .

When I was in eighth grade at Burbank Junior High School, I ate lunch each day with a group of girls who were casual friends of mine. The close friends I normally ate with had different lunch periods that semester, so this was the next best thing. Most of the girls at our lunch table were what you would call "popular," although I thought a couple of them were real snobs.

One day, Wanda showed up at our table. Now, I grew up far from the lap of luxury, but even by my standards Wanda was poor. Her clothes were terrible. Her lunches were pitiful. Sometimes, she even looked dirty. I guess she began sitting at our table because she wanted to belong to a group of girls she admired, but I'm not sure there was much to admire at that table. I always offered her a seat by me and tried to include her in the conversation as much as I could.

Most of us brought lunch from home, but getting at least one thing from the "lunch line" every day was considered the thing to do. Our favorite "extras" were mashed potatoes or a Mr. Goodbar—don't ask me why.

Before long, the girls at the table began to send Wanda to fetch their side orders for the day. She became like a little servant.

"Here Wanda," one of them would say, handing her money. "Go get me a Mr. Goodbar."

Although she could never afford any for herself, she would dutifully get up, walk to the lunch line, stand there for as long as it took, and bring back a tray of food. I watched this for a while, always wishing Wanda would say, "No, do it yourself." But she never did.

One day, I couldn't stand it any longer.

"She's not your servant," I blurted. "Go get your own food."

Wanda looked at me. The girls looked at me. And, one by one, they got up and started toward the line.

I'm sure the "popular" girls thought I was crazy. And I KNOW Wanda thought I was crazy, but I didn't care. She deserved to be treated better than that, even if she didn't think so.

I've always wondered what happened to Wanda. I've always wondered if she ever learned to tell people who wanted to take advantage of her, "No." If nothing else, I hope she's a little choosier about who she eats lunch with.

Why do we have popularity contests?

Who are the "popular" kids at your school? What kind of people are they? What are their values? What do they believe in? Does anybody even care?

Can someone tell me why we aren't a little pickier when it comes to naming our "best"? When it's time to elect "Miss Barfdale High," why do we always choose the girl with the biggest wardrobe or the cutest little face? What in the far blue yonder do those things have to do with choosing someone who is supposed to represent the best in all of us? Can't we see beyond such silliness?

Why do we vote for people who are disgustingly friendly to us when they are running for cheerleader but who never speak to us any other time? Why don't we have the nerve to tell them to take their pom-poms and "shoo"?

Why do we even have popularity contests? All they do is stroke the egos of a few kids and make everyone else feel like an unwanted growth. Is there a point to electing the "best dressed"? As if everyone in school doesn't already know that this "clothes person" keeps a spare bed at the mall, now you get to be reminded of it every time you open your yearbook.

I once saw a high school yearbook that pictured the SAME girl for "Miss Redbrick High School," "Most Likely to Succeed," "Best Dressed," and "Best All Around." Do you believe this? I asked, "What's the matter? Doesn't anybody else go to this school?"

I think it's time for you to make some changes. How about an honor for the kid with the weirdest lunches, or a vote for the guy with the most warts? How about that girl with the constant nasal drip, can't we give her something? These make about as much sense as some of the honors we give now.

We're talking about a major change here. Think about it.

Do siblings fit in a chapter on friendship?

Siblings are brothers, sisters, step-brothers, step-sisters, half-brothers and half-sisters. Well, experts call them "siblings"—most of the rest of us call them "pure torture." Living in the same house with these people can be like living through continuous re-runs of "Poltergeist." But look at it this way: These are the people you will probably be eating Thanksgiving dinner with for the rest of your life. You might as well make the best of it.

Most of us have gotten the wrong idea about the relationships we have with brothers and sisters. The truth of the matter is, we are given no choices in the deal, no chance to look them over ahead of time—nothing. They just sort of come with the house. And, like it or not, we'll continue to have a relationship with them for the rest of our lives. And you can believe that it will be like no other relationship ever.

Now, don't kid yourself, just because THEIR parents happen to be YOUR parents doesn't mean we're talking love at first sight. Brothers and sisters have been fighting with each other since the beginning of time over castles, inheritances, who gets to ride in the front seat, you name it.

If you want a good relationship with your siblings, the first thing you need to do is forget this stuff about loving them "just because they are family." I mean, it sounds nice and it works okay by the time you're about 40 years old, but when you're young, it's just not that simple. A few lucky brothers and sisters have this warm kind of natural schmooze between them and are simply goo-goo over each other, but most of us have to work real hard at getting along. If you don't want indigestion for the rest of your Thanksgiving dinners, you might try the following:

- Try to accept them for what they are.
- Don't expect them to be, think, or act just like you.
- Give them their space, just as you want yours.
- Try not to say horrible little things to them, try to be nice to them instead.
- Don't take their stuff without asking, say things like, "May I borrow your such-and-such?"
- Try to be on their side, at least part of the time.
- Above all, don't tattle unless it's a matter of life and death.

All of your efforts to become friends with your brothers and sisters will pay off in the long run. And even though it may seem impossible now, they just may end up becoming the dearest and closest friends you will ever have. I would never have believed it when I was 16, but my two sisters, Barbara and Claudia, have become my dearest friends. And do we ever love Thanksgiving dinner!

Southern accents and Queen Elizabeth . . .

I recently recorded a video series for teenage girls. In eight shows, I talk about many of the things you've read about in this book—self-esteem, relationships, values. The series is being used in schools . . . maybe you've seen it.

An interesting thing happened when samples of the taped shows were sent out for educators and other experts to watch, so they could decide if they wanted to buy the series for their school. Quite often, schools from the northern states sent back my videos with notes that read, "Her material is great, but we don't like her southern accent."

I *am* from the south. Not only from the south, but from Texas! To say I have a southern accent is to say water is wet. Now, when many people hear a southern accent, they immediately figure that the person speaking is mentally handicapped. It's prejudice. It's discrimination! It's unfair!

The reason I speak the way I do is because I was born in Texas. If I had been born in London, I'd sound like Queen Elizabeth. Big deal. The reason I am white is because I was born white. The reason my friend Rose is black is because she was born black. The reason my friend Delores is Hispanic is because she was born Hispanic. So what?

When in the world will we start accepting each other simply for what we are—no more, no less. Back in the '60s, my generation had a lot to say about civil rights and equality for all people. And some changes were made, but not enough. It's your turn now and best of luck to you. And could you do something about how folks feel about a southern accent?

Your life will never be the same . . .

Do you have friends with a skin color different from yours? If you're white, do you have black friends? If you're black, do you have brown friends? If you're brown, do you have white friends? If the answer if no, go find some new friends.

Do you have friends who are not of your religion? Do you have Catholic friends? Protestant friends? Muslim friends? Jewish friends? If not, go find some.

Do you have friends who don't live in your neighborhood? Do you have friends who don't go to your school? Do you have friends who don't go to your church? Do you have friends who don't do exactly what you do? If not, then go find some.

Don't shut yourself up in a closet of ignorance. Open your mind and your heart to new people—people who don't happen to be like you. Your life will never be the same.

We all need our friends . . .

Friendship has a funny way of being a lot of different things. For some people, it means hardly ever being apart, and for others it's being together only once in a while. Whatever works for you, I hope your friendships are full of loyalty, acceptance, honesty, equality, and thoughtfulness. But, most of all, I hope they are full of good influence.

Care for each other. Watch out for each other. It can be a cruel world out there. We all need our friends.

Section III

Boys: Parts I & II

Are you ready for this? There's one four-letter word no teenage girl can go very long without saying... "boys." And what a powerful word it can be. The very mention of it can ruin your day or make it the most exciting day you have ever lived. Isn't that incredible?

How can a boy make you bouncing-off-the-walls happy one minute and ready to commit murder the next? Why is it that being around that certain male human can bring out the very best in you . . . or the very worst? Relationships with boys—what a subject!

Sit back and hold on...

In the next two chapters, I'm going to tell you everything I can possibly think of on the subject of boys. Settle in, this may take a while.

I believe there are two separate sides in the relationships you have with guys, and that they are as different as Swiss and Cheddar. One is the fun, light-hearted side of the deal—flirting, meeting, phoning, note-writing, dating, dancing, winking, kissing, picnicking, having long talks, walking in the park . . . stop me when you've heard enough.

I call this side "romance". Then, there is the much more serious side of the story, the side that happens if the two of you ever decide to become sexually active. Not that sex isn't fun. It can be fun, that's why so many people keep getting into trouble because of it.

But let's take first things first and begin our look into relationships with boys back at the point when you first place an eyeball on one that's just to-die-for. After all, that's how the whole thing gets started, isn't it?

Six

Boys, Part I . . . Romance

When I was about 13 years old, I took a trip on a train with my daddy and my sisters, to Dallas to visit Aunt Evelyn and Uncle Marshall. We'd been on the train for about 15 seconds when I spotted two guys I thought were some kind of cute. They looked to be "college men," which made it all the more exciting. I managed to walk past them about 97 times and was headed for number 98 when the train suddenly lurched and I fell right across their laps. I wanted to die. It wouldn't have been so bad if they'd acted decent about the whole thing. But, noooo, they were total jerks. They laughed at me and suggested I go back to my seat and stay there.

It never dawned on me until many years later that they'd actually noticed the 97 trips I had made down the aisle of the train, grinning at them each time I walked by. What a stupid little nit they must have thought I was. And they were right. Chasing boys is a fine art, an art that is quickly disappearing from the face of the Earth.

Best friend to the rescue . . .

Let's say you have just discovered Mr. To-Die-For (let's call him Mr. TDF). He is so cute you can hardly breathe. Just seeing him walking down the hall at school makes you want to fall into your locker. You find yourself thinking about him constantly. And inside your brain, the computers are hastily working to find an answer to that all important question . . . "Is he available?"

At this point, 99.9 percent of all the teenage girls who have ever lived on Earth would move directly to Step #1 of the official How to Catch a Boy Policy. They'd send their best friend to find out everything she possibly could. They'd instruct that friend to be sure to ask all of the right questions: Is he going out with anybody? Well, does he LIKE anybody? Is he open to suggestions?

If *your* best friend returns with good news, let the games begin. And get ready for the next big question.

Does he have a pulse?

The second big question is . . . "How do I get Mr. TDF to notice me?" Well, falling into your locker is a start. Unless this guy is from another time warp, he probably already has a tiny suspicion that you are interested. After all, your best friend has been in his face asking a zillion questions—sure sign of a romance about to strike.

So you go into action and try any or all of the following:

- You make eye contact with him as often as possible.
- When you do catch his eye, you look right into those baby blues and say "Hi."
- You smile at him a lot.
- You walk by his locker.
- You start sitting near his lunch table.

- You show up in the places you know he'll be.
- You sit close to him in assembly programs.
- You get to know his friends.

Finally, there's no doubt that he's noticed you. He's seen you and knows you're around, so now what? It's time for the third big question.

Is he conscious?

The third big question is . . . "How do you actually talk with Mr. TDF?" Always remember, the best way to start a conversation is by asking a question.

You might try some of the following:

- "Are you going to the game Friday night?"
- "Do you know the homework assignment in Algebra? I missed it."
- "Did you hear what happened to Dexter Jones?" (Something better have happened to old Dexter if you use this one.)
- "Don't we live on the same street?" (Of course not, but you can always ask.)
- "Is that your locker?" (No, he's just standing there because there's a breeze.)
- "Does your little brother go to Nightmare Middle School? I think he's in my sister's class."
- "Don't you work at Burger Barf on weekends?"

You get the idea.

So you've found this guy, chased him down, and forced a conversation on him. What's next? I'll bet you think it's time to move on to the fourth big question, don't you? Well, it's not. The time for questions is over. Now, it's time for some real action.

But first, a thought here . . .

So far so good in the pursuit of Mr. TDF, don't you agree? Things are rocking along and appear to be right on course. But have you noticed something here? You (representing the female side of the relationship) seem to be doing all of the work. Why is that?

It's a well-known fact that girls usually mature faster than boys. Which means that girls begin to think about certain things a bit sooner than boys do—things like romance, for instance. So while some girls are ready to settle down and get married by the time they are 4, most guys are fully content to hang out with their buddies and play some sort of ball well into their 50s. It's not unusual for boys to need a little push when it comes to relationships with girls. In fact, it's quite normal. However, this does present us with a very special problem.

How do we do all this pushing and still hang on to our dignity? This is a very important question. Unfortunately, it's one we've stopped asking ourselves and are worse off because of it. Until recently, females gave a huge amount of thought to maintaining their dignity even though they were in the middle of a manhunt. Though maybe feeling wild and crazy over some guy, the idea was to take great pains to make him think you barely knew he was alive!

I remember hearing my mother's single women friends say, "Let him chase you until you catch him." I thought they were crazy until I got old enough to realize what they were talking about. They simply meant it was fine to show an interest in a guy but NEVER to chase one.

Now don't get me wrong, I'm not suggesting we never speak to a guy unless we are spoken to first. This chapter will prove that. But aggressive, pushy females are getting to be old news. I'm sick of seeing girls and women portrayed in movies and television shows as easy pushovers. And I think it's time we change that reputation we seem to have made for ourselves.

How do we do that? Never fear, I've got a plan.

Patty's "magic formula" for dealing with boys . . .

In your relationships with boys, there always comes that moment when you've done enough. There comes a time when it's your turn to sit back and give that particular boy a chance to make things work. Unfortunately, it's not that easy to know when the moment has arrived. And that's because girls love to take charge of things, make things happen, and see to all the details. We're such handy little fixers. Only sometimes, we don't know when it's time to stop "fixing," especially when it comes to the boys we love.

Have you ever known a girl who was so in love with some poor schmuck that she chased him and threw herself at him until he practically had to move to another state? Everybody else seemed to know that he wasn't interested in her. Everybody else got the message that he wanted her to leave him alone—everybody, that is, except her. "Well, that would never happen to me," you say. "I'd never be that stupid over a boy." Famous last words!

Love does funny things to us. It makes dodos out of geniuses. And believe me, making fools out of themselves over men has been a hobby with women since the beginning of time. So, what can we do? There has to be some kind of guideline we can go by, a map to keep us on course, so to speak. There must be something to help us when we fall for a guy and our brains go off to space camp

Well, worry no more, help is on the way. It's my magic formula, proven beyond any doubt to maintain dignity and pride. Use this formula, and you will always know when you've done enough and it's his turn to start giving. Memorize it. Believe in it. Live by it.

Here it is: "EVERY ACTION DESERVES AN EQUAL REACTION."

"Every action deserves an equal reaction" . . .

It may not be the formula to rid you of those cellulite thighs, but it can sure help solve your problems with boys. The idea is simple, and it all goes back to "balance." When you make an action toward a boy, you deserve an equal reaction from him—that is, if he's interested.

For instance, let's talk about that second big question—getting Mr. TDF to notice you. As you remember, we decided you could look, smile, follow, talk, show up, and sit close by in order to get his attention. When you do these things you are making an "action" toward him. Now, according to the formula, after you have put forth all of this effort, you deserve to receive an equal reaction from him.

In other words, if you say "hi" to him several times, it then becomes his turn to say "hi" to you. If you walk by his locker, he should walk by your locker.

And if he's interested in you, that's exactly what he'll do.

Pizza and a video sounds good to me . . .

The thing that's so great about my formula is that it helps you to know what your behavior should be in almost any situation where a boy is concerned—like calling a guy on the phone, for instance. I'll bet you've already had a discussion or two with your mom on this very subject. And, unless I miss my guess, she was probably strongly opposed to you making such a call. Most moms feel this way.

Let me tell you why. When your mother was young (back before the wheel was invented), "nice" girls did not call boys on the telephone. It just wasn't done. Any girl who called boys soon found herself with a racy reputation. We "nice" girls sat at home by the phone for hours waiting for the little goons to call us, and we wasted many a good day that way.

To be honest, I think your approach to the problem is much more intelligent than ours. After all, you could reach retirement age before some of these guys snap out of their confusion long enough to make a phone call. So if you want to talk with him and feel the time is right, why not give him a little jingle? It makes perfect sense to me. (I tell moms this every chance I get.)

The issue is not who calls who first. The issue is BALANCE. Here's where the formula comes in. If you call a boy, you've made an *action* toward him. You now deserve an equal reaction from him. He should call you. And if he doesn't, forget him.

The formula can help you figure out other situations, too. Inviting a boy to your house for pizza and a video is fine, but the next invitation should come from him.

Are you always the one who shows up where he'll be? Let him follow *you* around for a while. The formula helps you keep things balanced, equal, and fair. It's all right to give a boy a little shove toward romance, just make sure you're not shoving with an 18-wheeler.

Testing the balance . . .

Romance is like walking a tightrope, and balance is the key to survival. If you do all of the giving, arranging, talking, or chasing, you'll fall flat on your face. And the same thing is true for a boy. But, for reasons we've already discussed, boys are usually not into "chasing" as much as girls are, especially during the teen years. The idea just hasn't quite hit them yet. They're more into making foul noises and grossing people out.

Gross as they can be, we still manage to fall head over heels in love with them, don't we? The big question we have to ask ourselves is, "Is he as 'in love' with me as I am with him?" When a boy is interested in a relationship with you, you don't have to hunt him down like he's an escaped convict. He will almost always participate willingly.

If there is a special boy in your life right now, ask yourself the following questions to see if the relationship you have with him is a balanced one.

- Does he show as much interest in the relationship as you do?
- Does he phone you as often as you phone him?
- Does he find you at school as often as you find him?
- Are the things you do together balanced?
- If you go out on dates, do you share in deciding where you will go and what you will do?
- If you write love notes to him or send him cards, do you ever receive such things in return?
- Do you spend time with your friends as well as his?
- If you do something that he's interested in (such as going to a sports event), is he then happy to do something you want to do (such as attending a family get-together)?

If the answer to any of these questions is "No," you should give some very serious thought to where this relationship is headed.

Let the flirting begin . . .

I don't know why "flirting" has gotten such a bad name. I think it is positively wonderful. After all, it's nothing more than being friendly. At least, it shouldn't be any more than that.

Now, "teasing"—that's something else entirely. Girls who tease seem to be promising something they may or may not want to deliver. Teasing is more of a sexual game. It usually involves a lot of touching, sexual comments, and leading moves. Boys don't like to be teased and usually don't have very high opinions of the girls who do it.

Flirting is different. Flirting is smiling, saying "hi," making eye contact and not being afraid to let a boy know you just might be interested. Boys love for you to flirt with them. It lets them know you've noticed them and that you like what you see. There is nothing wrong with that.

This time, it's his turn . . .

As you know by now, I think it's perfectly okay for you to make an "action" toward a boy. We've already discussed things like talking to him, phoning him, and even inviting him over before he had made the same kind of move toward you. But what about actually asking a guy out for a date? Should this be just another step in your "take charge" attitude about the things that affect your life?

Let's look at this question very closely. Usually, by the time two teens actually get to the dating stage, a lot has already taken place. There have been those first conversations, telephone calls, casual stops by your house, and so on. Most teen couples have created some sort of relationship, even if it's a small one, before they decide to spend an entire evening together. It isn't as if a date occurs the first time you lay eyes on each other—as is often the case with adults who are playing the dating game.

If you use my formula, by the time all this "action" has taken place, you already know that he's interested in you or you wouldn't still be involved with him. Okay, since there's mutual interest on both sides, why not let *him* ask for that first date? Call me a little old-fashioned on this one, but it seems to me, for your own reputation and honor, this is the best way to go on this subject.

There will be those occasions when asking a boy out first is the sensible thing to do—for a special family event or to have a date for something that you are involved in—say your dad's birthday barbecue or the student council picnic. But once you have invited him to something, it is definitely his turn to ask you out next. NEVER EVER ask him out a second time. That's just TOO tacky.

Princess Di and you . . .

"Rejection" has to be one of the yuckiest words ever invented, but it's a word we can quickly become familiar with once we allow ourselves to indulge in any sort of romance. Even the most talented and beautiful women imaginable have faced the pain of being rejected by the men they love. No matter who you are, how beautiful you may be or how much money you may possess, rejection hurts.

Most of us have heard the stories about Prince Charles's affair with "the OTHER woman." Who knows if the tales are true or not, but I figure if it can happen to Princess Di, the rest of us don't stand a chance. Dealing with rejection is something we should all give a little thought to.

Let's say you have been going with Mr. TDF for a while now. Life couldn't be sweeter. But, now that you think about it, there may have been a few tell-tale signs lately that all is not well. Standing in front of your locker one day, practically in front of the whole student body, Mr. TDF tells you he doesn't want to go together anymore. He needs some space and, for right now, wants the two of you to be "friends." (I hate it when they say they just want to be "friends," don't you?) So there you stand with your face hanging all over the floor, your liver in a knot and your toes curled backward, and off he walks . . . the love of your life, the man of your dreams, the scumbag of the world.

At this point, you probably do what any decent

woman in love does. You bounce into a severe case of hysteria accompanied by screams and seizures (Boo-hoo-hoo-hoo, Waah-waah-waah). It gets pretty ugly. A crowd gathers and the whole day is shot.

Why do we girls react to rejection this way? I know, I know—it's because our hearts are broken and we've lost our one true love. But is it really necessary to feel like life is over because some boy chooses to spend his time elsewhere?

Let's think about this rationally for a moment.

In the course of your life, you will (I hope) date many guys, with each relationship starting off very exciting and full of possibilities. As the days pass and you continue to develop and grow as a person, you will find that this guy or that guy is not exactly what you're looking for. So you'll break the ties that have developed between the two of you and move on. Isn't that the perfectly sane thing to do? Why would you stay with someone who is not right for you? Only people with bad emotional problems do that. Now, we can accept this quite easily when it is WE who are doing the choosing, but when a boy chooses to break up with us, we go bonkers.

Why not look at it this way? When faced with rejection, rather than deciding you'll never draw another breath, why not tell yourself the following: "This is okay. It is time to move on. I have learned from this relationship. I am a better and stronger person because of it. And I will now be able to find an even better relationship with the next person who comes my way. Even though he was the one who chose to leave, that doesn't mean there is something wrong with me. It only means that we've grown apart, and he was the first to see it. And, anyway, he won't find someone like me on every corner. I'll be the one he tells his grandchildren about someday. With tears in his eyes, he'll tell them the story of 'The Girl I Lost'. Ha! That'll serve him right. I shall now move forward to find someone 10 times better than he was. In fact, I feel better already."

Okay, so the whole speech sounds like a crock, but it's better than kicking in the walls of your bedroom. Just remember, we all have our hearts broken sooner or later. Once someone in a relationship wants it to be over, no matter what the other person does, it's pretty well over. So if that's the case and the boy you're going out with decides to call it quits, why not go out with your head held high and your vocal cords still working? Dignity, remember, dignity. It won't be long before you discover there is something much better coming your way. Trust me.

What a web we weave . . .

When I was a teen, Neil Sedaka came out with his megahit "Breakin' Up Is Hard To Do." Every teenager who went through a break-up during that time wailed and moaned while singing along with Neil. In the words of that song, he spoke for all of us. Breaking up IS hard to do, especially when the relationship has been around for a while.

From the moment you choose to become involved in a relationship with a boy, bonds are formed that tie the two of you closer and closer together—the first phone call, the first note written, the first visit to your home, the first introduction to family, the first touch, the first kiss. All of these become like small threads that weave together the fabric of your relationship. And the more time you spend together and the more things you do together, the more threads are added to the fabric. Soon, you become like two spiders caught in a web. If the relationship is balanced and good, it can be a cozy little nest you find yourselves in, one that will protect the two of you when the harsh winds of life howl around you. But if the relationship is one that needs to be ended, each of those ties will have to be severed before either of you can go free. And that will take time and a great deal of strength.

Sometimes, even when we know a relationship should

be over, we don't end it because we aren't brave enough to cut the ties. It seems much easier to remain in the stillness of the web. But webs can be deceiving, and they can be a trap. They can kill that spark within you that seeks the best and hopes for the most out of life.

Don't live your life tied by old bonds that no longer bring you happiness. Neil Sedaka may have been wrong. Breakin' up isn't nearly as hard as living miserably.

But he's so shy . . .

I was out shopping with my daughter Stephanie one day when I got this great brainstorm about relationships with boys. Actually, I've spent many days shopping with my Steph. She's five-foot three-inches tall and weighs 99 pounds, so finding clothes that fit her well can be a royal headache. It's kind of like shopping for a human Barbie Doll. It wasn't so bad when she was a junior miss, but now that she's grown and married, she wants clothes that look a bit more sophisticated. She must have tried on 4,000 outfits as we trudged through every shop in the mall. I stopped counting after my feet fell off. Some of the outfits that I thought were fine, she turned down. "It's just not what I'm looking for, Mother," she'd say.

Finally, we stopped for a cup of coffee and began to talk about all the clothes we'd seen that day. It suddenly hit me how choosy we can be over a new dress. We'll reject it for any number of small reasons no one else would probably even notice: The color is wrong, it doesn't fit quite right in the waistline, the sleeves are too short, the collar too big. On and on we go, in search of the perfect thing to wear, and we don't give up until we find exactly what we're looking for.

Wouldn't it be wonderful if we were only *half* that choosy about the guys we decide to become involved with? When it comes to them, we aren't picky enough. We close our eyes to the truth and make one excuse after another for the way they treat us.

He doesn't call when he says he will? Yes, but he's so funny. He doesn't treat you that great in front of his friends? Yes, but his eyes are so blue. He only wants to do what suits him on a date? Yeah, but he brought me roses that time. He's sometimes rude to you? Yes, but he doesn't really mean it. He's always staring at other girls when he's out with you? Yeah, but he's just a guy, and guys can't help looking at girls.

Give me a break.

Can you imagine seeing a cute dress hanging on a rack, taking it to the dressing room, trying it on and—even though it's too big and too long, or too short and too tight—buying it anyway? Why in the world would you do that? Because it's so cute hanging on the rack? Wouldn't it matter at all that it wasn't right for you? Wouldn't it be important that the dress was never going to make you happy and that you'd always end up feeling bad every time you wore it?

The next time you find yourself making excuses for that boyfriend of yours, imagine that he's a dress. Then ask yourself if you shouldn't just keep on shopping.

Young love . . .

LOVE. We sing songs about it. We leave home for it. We think we can't live without it.

Many people think teens like you don't really fall in love—not REALLY in love. They say you suffer from infatuation or, better yet, "puppy love." As if you are a bunch of dogs. Well, they're dead wrong. Teens do fall in love—deeply and honorably in love. And your love is as real as anything you've known so far.

When you experience love as a teen, you feel the same thrills and pains anyone has felt who has ever been in love. It may not last forever, but while it's here, it's real. You may not be able to feel the commitment of a relationship that has lasted for years and been through all sorts of ups and downs, but you do know what it's like to be committed to the ups and downs of a relationship that has lasted a few weeks or months. It's kind of like driving a car. When you first start driving, you may not be as experienced or react as quickly as a person who has been driving for 20 years, but you still know how to drive.

I think young love may be stronger in some ways than the love older people experience, because the feelings are so new, so unlike anything you've ever felt before. These new feelings can totally overwhelm you. They can knock you right off your feet. And, whether you're young or old, falling in love feels good—and it feels horrible. It's all the things you dream it will be and not at all what you expect. It's complicated, but simple; confusing, yet plain as the nose on your face. And, most of all, it's one of the grandest parts of the "change".

Enjoy.

And when you're not looking . . .

Do you want to know the secret to finding a boyfriend? A GREAT boyfriend? Well, I'm going to tell you for once and for all, the low-down you've been dying to hear.

STOP LOOKING!

Forget it.

Don't think about it.

Instead, concentrate on you. Turn all that concern toward yourself, your own goals, your own dreams and your own plans for the rest of your life. Forget about boys. Forget about dates. Forget about who you will be with next. Think instead about how you can create a life for yourself that is happy and full. Develop friendships with other girls. Make plans with them. Go places together.

Look forward to activities you can enjoy with them. Stay busy. Exercise. Learn to sew. Paint your bedroom. Take a cooking class. Learn a foreign language. Volunteer at the local hospital. Plant a garden.

Create a life that is full of energy and contentment, and boys will be drawn to you—not because you are conniving and plotting ways to get their attention—but because they can't help but notice a girl whose life is so together.

The really neat guys are looking for a girl just like this—a girl who knows and believes in herself, a girl who is not afraid to walk alone until the right guy comes along. And that girl should be *you*!

Have you ever been in love?

Maybe you're in love now. It's a neat feeling, isn't it? It hits you right in the pit of your stomach and bounces off your insides like a cosmic flash.

Have you ever thought about how many times you've been in love before? (Once . . . 10 times . . . 50 times?) Why not take a minute and think of all those former "loves." Each time the love seemed to be very real, didn't it?

Remember how strong your feelings were for that certain boy who seemed to be everything you wanted? Remember how you thought that this was going to be the guy for you forever? How do you feel about him today? Do you wonder what you ever saw in him? Do you think of him now and find it hard to believe that you liked him as much as you did?

It might have been all right for Sleeping Beauty to latch on to the first guy who kissed her, but it just doesn't work *these* days. Love can change so quickly on us. What appears true and real today can be like a puff of smoke tomorrow. Feelings that are so strong they seem to come from inside the very deepest part of your soul can disappear before your eyes . . . "poof"!

Will you believe me when I tell you that the feelings you call "love" today can and will happen again and again to you in your lifetime? And someday, when you are ready and the time is right, you will find a very special someone who will be just the person you want to share your life with.

Until then, don't let love fool you. Don't be so in love with love that you grab the first boy who comes along. Don't be so desperate to have a boy in your life that you settle for less than you deserve. Slow down. Take your time. Relax. There are lots of boys on this planet. And you are just getting started.

Only when you discover YOU . . .

One thing that I hope you have learned from this chapter is that you will never find your value as a person or your purpose for life in a BOY—no matter how hard you try!

You can only find these things within YOURSELF. There are many women my age who still don't know this, and they keep jumping from man to man hoping someday they will find someone to make them feel valuable and happy. And it never happens.

Love is wonderful. It can bring happiness into your life, but only if there is BALANCE in the relationship, and only if you bring to the relationship a strong understanding of YOURSELF.

If your generation of young women could learn this and live by it, the future for all mankind would be changed and the things that now make us weak as a society would change into things that make us strong again. Marriages would have a chance for survival, divorce might become rare again, and children could grow up in families that stay together.

These changes could really happen. You have the power to make them happen. Look within yourself. There you will find your value. And when you have discovered YOU, you will then be ready to find Mr. To-Die-For.

Seven

Boys, Part II . . . Sex

Boys are different than girls. Okay, okay, you already know that. But, I mean, they are REALLY different, especially when it comes to SEX.

In the movie "City Slickers," Billy Crystal's character sums up how males and females view sex differently when he says, "Women need a reason, men just need a place."

When it comes to sex, men don't think like we think. They don't feel the things we feel, they don't want the same things we want. They're different. Try to get this into your head. Let it sink in for just a moment. We are talking apples and oranges here—different.

This is nothing new. It's been this way for as long as anybody can remember. Not that we females have been quick to accept the fact. We've always had a tough time with this one. Oh, we know the differences are there—opposite ways of thinking, different views on almost everything. But in the back of our minds we figure that this is not such a big problem because we can FIX it. We can make everything all right. We'll simply CHANGE them. Yeah, that's it, we'll CHANGE the boys so that they'll be like us. HA!

It's never happened and it never will.

Two different tales . . .

Did you ever see the movie "Grease"? It's a musical. I love musicals. Those are the movies where people jump around dancing and singing to each other. Actually, they're ridiculous but I still love them. Anyway, there is a song in "Grease" that makes the point about these male-female differences better than anything I've ever heard.

In the film, the story goes that Sandy and Danny meet at the beach while on summer vacation. They fall in love but have to say goodbye at the end of summer, not realizing that they'll be attending the same school in the fall. The first day of school, before they've seen each other, they tell their friends about their exciting summer romance. Danny is sitting in the bleachers with his buddies, and Sandy, who's new to the school, is sitting in the cafeteria with a group of girls. The scene goes back and forth between Sandy and Danny who, although singing the same song, are telling two very *different* stories. Listen to their words:

Sandy: "Summer lovin', happened so fast."
Danny: "Summer lovin', had me a blast."
Sandy: "Met a boy, cute as can be."
Danny: "Met a girl, crazy for me."
Girls: "Tell me more, like, does he have a car?"
Boys: "Tell me more, did you get very far?"
Sandy: "He ran by me, got my suit damp."
Danny: "She swam by me, she got a cramp."
Sandy: "He showed off, splashing around."

Danny: "I saved her life, she nearly drowned."
Girls: "Tell me more, was it love at first sight?"
Boys: "Tell me more, did she put up a fight?"
Sandy: "We stayed out, 'til ten o'clock."
Danny: "We made out, under the dock."
Sandy: "He got friendly, holding my hand."
Danny: "She got friendly, down in the sand."
Sandy: "He was sweet, just turned eighteen."
Danny: "She was good, know what I mean?"

Here we have two people who had the very same experience, but you'd never know it to hear the two different stories they tell. Boys are different. It's a fact.

The time for fairy tales is over . . .

If I can get you, at the very beginning of this chapter on sex, to accept the fact that guys don't think, act, or feel as you do when it comes to sexual matters, we may be able to make a little progress here.

I wish I could tell you how many conversations I've had with teenage girls across this country who have had sex and ended up wishing they hadn't. Their words to me always begin with "If I had only known . . . " or "But, he said . . . " or "I never thought . . . "

This ignorance about the reality of boys needs to stop! And if you read this chapter carefully and with an open mind, you will never be ignorant about them again.

The time for fairy tales is over. Thousands of teenage girls like you are being hurt every single day because they still believe in fairy tales when it comes to boys and sex.

Here is a perfect example: I was speaking at a large high school in Florida and, after the program, a very attractive girl came up and said she had to talk to me in private. The girl said that she was 16 and had fallen in love with a boy at her school who was 18. She had been crazy about him for years, but, for the longest time, he never knew she was alive. Once she began to grow up—hair long, makeup just right, skirts very short—she got his attention. She chased him, called him, and always showed up where he would be. Finally, he asked her out.

What do you think he wanted to do on their very first date? That's right, they had sex together. She was so crazy about him, she wasn't about to tell him no. And, anyway, she thought he would now be hers. Surely he loved her. After all, didn't the sex they'd shared mean something? But it didn't quite work out that way.

The next day she waited all day for the phone to ring, but he never called. And at school on Monday, he didn't even speak to her. In fact, she saw him walking down the hall with another girl. That night, she cried herself to sleep—the next night, too, and the next. Finally she decided to call him. Maybe there had been a misunderstanding, she thought. When he answered, she began to cry. She told him how much she loved him and that she would do anything to hold on to him. He basically told her he wasn't interested.

"Now what?" she asked me. She had even thought about suicide. I've heard the same story a thousand times. It's time for a change.

A lot of "peaking" going on . . .

Human beings are not like math problems. One rule doesn't fit all. So when we try to explain human behavior, we usually go by what MOST people do. Most of us go through a sexual "peak" at some point in our lives. A sexual peak is a period of time when a person thinks about, cares about, and wants sex more than at any other time.

Boys usually reach their peak in their late teens to early 20s. Some reach it sooner, and some later. What this means is that teenage boys think about sex a lot. My estimate is every 11 seconds, but I may be wrong. It may be more often than that. I can promise you that *he* thinks about it more than *you* do, because women reach their sexual peak at about age 30—give or take a day or two.

This does not mean that all guys are sex freaks. It simply means that they are going through a very normal and natural stage of their lives. None of us have any control over when our bodies decide it's time to peak. The hormones just start bouncing around and off we go. It isn't like we plan it. It just happens.

We have to understand this and be honest enough with ourselves to admit that, while a boy is "peaking-out," he is very driven by a sexual desire that can override his good common sense. And when that boy happens to be your favorite fella, you can have your work cut out for you. If you aren't strong enough to handle the situation, you can end up with a major problem. Because, while he may be the one peaking, you are the one with the most to lose.

In the deep end and sinking fast . . .

None of this "peaking" stuff has a thing to do with falling in love. Boys are not heartless little vultures who've been programmed to seek and destroy. Boys fall in love. They fall passionately and madly in love, just as you do. But when they fall in love, they are much more influenced by sexual thoughts and desires than you are.

Let's put it this way: Two non-swimmers fall into the same swimming pool, but one falls into the shallow end while the other falls into the deep end. Now, even though they fell into the same pool and neither of them can swim, they are NOT going to have the same experience, are they? The one in the deep end is going to have to work a lot harder to survive than the one in the shallow end, right?

Yes, boys fall in love. Yes, they are very capable of caring for the girls they love. But once sex enters into a relationship—usually at the boy's suggestion—it will be the girl who finds herself in deep water.

These numbers don't lie . . .

Every day, more than 3,000 teenage girls get pregnant in our country.

Every day, ZERO teenage boys get pregnant in our country.

Think about it.

3,000 pregnant girls . . .

Let's make the number 3,000 something you can see with your own eyes.

I want you to think about your school auditorium. Most high school auditoriums hold 700 to 800 people. Let's say yours hold 750. Now, in your mind's eye, stand on the stage in your auditorium and watch as the back doors swing open and 750 girls walk in to fill every seat in front of you. Can you see them? Now have them all stand and file out. Then have 750 more come in. Do this until you have filled that auditorium four times. *That* is 3,000!

Did you see their faces? Did you see the potential that sat there in front of you? Every day, 3,000 teenage girls, just like the ones you have pictured in your mind, get pregnant.

A new United Nations report says that American teenage girls have the highest rates of abortion, the highest rates of total pregnancies, and the highest birth rates in the modern, developed world—ten times higher than Japan, three times higher than in most European countries.

Don't you think it's time for change?

You will never find "balance" here . . .

If only the odds were a little more in your favor. If only half of the pregnancy would happen to you and the other half were the boy's responsibility—now, that would be a balanced deal. If only boys had monthly periods, like girls do. (Wouldn't that be a hoot . . . can you imagine a guy with cramps?) If only things were just a little more fair. But they're not. We have the babies—they don't. That's the bottom line.

What is the boy's place in all this merriment? How does he pay for those fun-filled hours in the back seat of the car? He marries his girl if she gets pregnant, of course. Right? I wondered about that myself, so I began to ask around. "How many boys stay with a girl once she gets pregnant?" Trust me, nobody has an answer to that one.

The only place where I could find a clue about what you can expect from your boyfriend should you get pregnant was from two women who deal with the problem every day. They both work in pregnancy clinics. The first told me this: "For every 100 girls who come into my clinic, I will see ONE boy."

I told that story to an audience of teenage girls at a large, inner-city high school. After the program, the second woman I mentioned came up to talk with me. She said, "Patty, I've worked in a teen pregnancy clinic for three years. We see 15 girls each day. That's 75 a week. I've *yet* to see the first boy walk into my clinic. But you know who is there with the girls? Their mothers."

Isn't this something? It takes two people to make a baby, but only one has to stick around to suffer the results—and that's you, teenage girl.

What kind of father would you be?

I wonder what would happen if it was the other way around? What if it were the BOYS who got pregnant? I wonder how many girls would stay faithful to them, stick by their men through the whole ordeal and offer to get married, or at least help support the baby?

How many girls would offer to drive their boyfriend to the doctor for his pre-natal check-ups, place a cool cloth on his head when the morning sickness was unbearable, be by his side as he walked down the halls at school, ignoring the whispers and rude remarks and hold his hand when he faced his angry and disappointed parents?

Do you think we would abandon them the way they usually abandon us? I wonder.

We try it, but it doesn't work . . .

When I want to know something about teenage girls, I always go directly to the ones who know the most about the subject—teenage girls like you. I wanted to know why, in spite of all they have to lose, teenage girls become sexually active.

My survey question (page) was, "Do you think most teenage girls who become involved in a sexual relationship do so because it's what they really want to do or because they think it's what the boy wants?" I thought at least half would say "It's what the girl really wants to do." But I was wrong.

Of the 7,000 girls I surveyed, 79 percent (that's 8 out of every 10 girls taking the survey) said they think it's *what the boy wants.*

Don't misunderstand this. Nobody is saying that girls never have a sexual thought and don't get pleasure from sexual contact. But the comments teenage girls made on this survey have said this:

"Look, when we have sex, it's usually not our idea. And, even if it is our idea, we are probably just trying to prove something to the guy—like, we can be just as wild and sexy as any other girl he might have in mind. And if being sexy is what it takes to get a guy and hold him, then that's what we will do."

What I find most interesting about this is that it doesn't work! Apparently we have become convinced through the years that sex is the way to hold a boy. But it's a lie.

Do you really believe that the girls who have sex with their boyfriends always manage to keep them? Can you count on a guy to stay true blue as long as you are sexually involved? Will he stay around once a baby is on the way? But, most important, are you willing to put your life, your future, on the line just to find out?

Smashed up and out of control . . .

You have a lot to lose in a sexual relationship—much more than a boy does. If these same odds were against you in any other area of your life, you would do everything you could to change it.

Let's say tomorrow morning the headlines read, "Due To New Female Virus, 1.2 Million Teenage Girls To Be Injured While Driving Autos This Year." As you scan the article for details, you read that a new virus has invaded the country, and it only affects teenage girls who are driving automobiles. The article states that, while driving, girls lose control, become involved in smashups, and end up injured—often for life.

Wouldn't you love to own a bicycle shop if such a story ran? You couldn't *pay* teenage girls to drive cars after such news. Girls everywhere would ride buses, take taxis, buy bicycles, hire drivers—what ever it took to avoid such pain and agony. And yet, day after day, night after night, teenage girls become smashed up and injured because of sex.

I don't think you've looked at being sexually active in

this way before. Most girls like you figure that sex is a two-way street. You may think that if you're old enough to decide that you want to be sexually active, it's no different for you than it is for the boy. After all, you're no baby anymore. You're a savvy gal. You can handle it.

I'm not surprised if you feel this way. Sex has been made to look so great in the movies we love, the TV shows we laugh at, the music we dance to and the advertisements we see. We've all been led to believe that any female worth her stuff is sexy and ready to take on any man she pleases. What a bunch of garbage. We've all been fooled.

It's time for us to snap out of our foolishness. We've talked throughout this book about balance. Where is the balance in teen sex? Where is the fairness? Sex is not the same for you as it is for boys, and all the "liberation" in the world will not change this fact.

On the next few pages, you will read, in very plain language, the *FOUR THINGS YOU HAVE TO LOSE IN A SEXUAL RELATIONSHIP* that a boy does not.

No matter what has happened to you in the past, no matter what is happening in your life at this moment, please read these next pages with an open mind. Tomorrow is a new day, a new beginning, a time for change.

Reputation . . .

Do you know a girl who has a reputation for "sleeping around"? She's an easy make and everybody knows it. She seems to be with a different guy every time you see her, and she's usually draped all over whoever she's with. People talk behind her back. They call her cheap and a "slut". Nobody bothers to ask why she might be doing these things, they just think she's trash.

Now, let's turn that question in another direction. Do

you know a boy who has a reputation for "sleeping around"? He's the guy who can't keep his hands off the ladies. It's not unusual to see him in the halls at school putting his line on many different girls, especially the young ones who don't know the score. He's a heartbreaker and a lover. He'll say whatever it takes to get a girl into bed with him. And most people look on him as a normal, average kind of guy.

Here we have a perfect example of two people who have built the same reputation for themselves, but the girl is a slut and the boy is just taking advantage of a good thing. After all, boys will be boys, right? The girl is scum, but the boy is macho. The girl should know better; the boy is just being a man.

It's called the old "double standard" and has been around for as long as anyone can remember. When it comes to reputation and sex, you have a lot more to lose than boys do, even though you're doing the very same thing.

The hidden threats of sexually transmitted disease . . .

The doctors call them STDs. But don't boys get sexually transmitted diseases too? Sure, but not like you do.

Because a boy's sexual organs are on the outside of his body, he can usually see if he has any kind of problem. All he has to do is open his eyes and look. But you're different. Because your sexual organs are on the inside of your body you can't see them, you often have no idea what's going on. You can catch an STD and not have a clue. Or the clue that you do have may go unnoticed or, worse, ignored.

Let's say, after sexual contact you develop an itching, redness, or slight discharge. You're certainly not eager to mention this to anyone, so you try to ignore it. Sure enough, a week or two later, it goes away. Whew, what a relief. It was probably nothing, you think. But it may have been something *very* important.

Like any other disease, the secret to fighting an STD is early treatment. The longer it goes untreated, the worse the result.

After sexual contact, if a boy suspects that he has a problem and goes to the doctor to receive treatment right away, he can be off and sailing in no time. You, on the other hand, may not even be aware that you have a problem; months can pass, maybe even years, and the results can be a *nightmare.*

Imagine that you are happily married and that you and your husband decide it's time to start a family. Unable to get pregnant, you go to the doctor.

"Well, Mrs. Jones, it's no wonder," the doctor shakes his head. "Your female organs have been destroyed by a sexually transmitted disease. Why didn't you get treatment? We could have helped you. Now, it's too late."

Here you are with a body full of disease and you are probably facing major surgery. Not only that, but there is little hope for children and you have a husband who wants to know what's going on. Boys get syphilis, gonorrhea, and herpes, just like girls do; but for girls, the outcome can be much worse.

There is one sexually transmitted disease which treats everyone somewhat equally - AIDS. I say SOMEWHAT equally because the newest studies indicate it is much easier for a female to get AIDS from a male than for a male to become infected from a female who is an AIDS carrier. Once again, we girls get to be the underdog.

What's most disturbing to me, however, is that teens are quickly becoming the new group hardest hit by the AIDS epidemic, something that experts have been telling us to expect for a while now. In large cities, one out of every 100 teens now carries the AIDS virus. That's a 40 percent increase in two short years.

We should find little comfort in the fact that AIDS treats males and females with equality because, you see, there really is no fairness in this battle with AIDS. All participants die.

Pregnancy . . .

Boys don't get pregnant—girls do. Boys don't get scared to death after they've "done it"—girls do. Boys don't frantically wait for their periods to start—girls do.

Boys don't wake up morning after morning so sick that they throw up their toenails—pregnant girls do. Boys don't have to go to those clinics for embarrassing and uncomfortable exams—girls do. Boys don't have to look their parents in the eye and say "I'm pregnant"—girls do. Boys don't watch as their bodies grow and bloat into something they no longer recognize, something so different from the small, youthful body they once had—girls do.

Boys don't listen to the snickers in the hallways at school as word gets around that they are "in trouble"—girls do. Boys don't give up all the fun, the running around with friends, and the partying because of a pregnancy—girls do. Boys don't worry over whether to have that abortion or not—girls do. Boys don't know the humiliation of a teen pregnancy—girls do. Boys don't cry themselves to sleep at night knowing that they have lost something they will never have again—girls do.

Boys don't get pregnant—girls do.

Facing tough choices . . .

If you become pregnant, you must make one of three choices. None of them are easy.

1. Have the baby and keep it.
2. Have the baby and put it up for adoption.
3. Have an abortion.

Let's say you get pregnant and decide that you are going to have the baby and keep it. And your boyfriend has taken a hike—that's what most girls find happens.

The first thing you get to do is deal with the heartbreak of knowing that his love for you was not true. That's not going to be easy, but let's say you've dealt with it and have come to grips with the fact that you are in this by yourself. Now you get to sit by while everyone else finds out about your little problem. Your parents, grandparents, brothers, sisters, aunts, uncles, neighbors, friends, and teachers will all find out. You can avoid this for a while, but once you begin to show, the news will travel fast.

Soon, you'll need to make some very important decisions. Do you quit school? Two out of three girls do, you know. Not me, you say? You are going to hang tough. Good for you, but that means you will continue attending classes even when the word gets out and everybody knows.

Maybe your school offers a special place for girls who are expecting a baby. Either way, it won't be easy. Going through a pregnancy never is, even under the best of circumstances. Morning sickness can be rough, and there will be days you can hardly stand the thought of going to class.

What about your health and the health of your baby? You must have prenatal care or you could be taking serious chances with your future and the future of your child. The average cost for prenatal care plus delivery is about the same as a new car these days. Who will pay for this?

What if there are complications and the bill is twice that amount? Maybe you'll need to have your baby at a charity hospital. It'll cost much less, but each time you go for a check-up you will wait in line for hours with other girls just like you. You'll probably see a different doctor each visit and you may or may not know the one who actually delivers your baby. You can't be too choosy when you take charity.

What about food and clothes for your baby after it's born? Will you buy these things? Maybe your parents will come up with the money. But, wait, they've already raised a family, haven't they? Now they get to start paying for your children, too? Does that seem fair?

Where will you get all of the things you need once you have a baby to care for? You'll need a high chair, stroller, crib, car seat, diapers, formula, toys, blankets, shoes . . . What about medicine? What if the baby gets sick? What if it needs to go to the hospital? Will you be able to see that your baby gets the best medical attention? In the face of all these needs, will you finally just give up and go on welfare? Will you let the government and all the other American people who work hard for their money pay for you and your baby?

What about you? Where will you get your clothes? What about a car? With little education, what kind of a job will you be able to find? And who will take care of your baby while you work? Will you be able to afford a babysitter? How will you find time to go out with friends? Babies need an awful lot of attention, you know.

What about dating? You will want to date again someday. What if you fall for a guy who doesn't care for the fact that you have a child by someone else? What if he's not very nice to your baby? Will you have the strength to tell him to get lost?

Does all of this sound like a little too much for you? Then maybe you should think about option number two: *adoption*. Let's take a look at what adoption is really about. First, you will go through much of what a girl who decides to keep her baby faces. You'll face the embarrassment, loneliness, people talking, decisions about school, and problems with money.

Then you'll spend nine long months feeling that baby grow and move and stretch inside of you. You'll even feel it hiccup. And during that nine months, you'll ask yourself a thousand questions. "What does it look like? What will its name be? Will it be like me? Will it be smart in school? Will it be funny? Will it be popular? Will it be successful someday? Will it wonder about me?"

But you may never know the answers to these questions, because, moments after the baby is born, it will be taken from you. And you will walk away from the hospital with empty arms. You will have given the baby life, but it will be a life that you will never have the honor of seeing. And every year on the baby's birthday, a day that will be burned into your memory forever, you will ask yourself all of those questions again. "What is the baby like? Is it happy? Does it look like me?"

But you will never know.

About 4 out of every 10 girls who become pregnant decide to get abortions. Some seem to think that it's the easy way out, but very few feel that way once it's done. From the moment you walk into an abortion clinic, your life is never the same again.

First, you fill out a few forms and talk with an advisor who wants you to be sure of the decision you are about to make. Then you'll be taken to the back room where you will climb up onto an abortion table, place your heels in two stirrups, and watch as you are connected to machines and tubes that will suck the child you carry out of your body.

Make no mistake, the child you carry inside you at that moment is a living being. But it will be dead before this procedure is over. That is a fact. You will be scared. You will cry and bleed. And soon you will be sent home to mend. Only you never will. Your body may heal, but your mind will carry the abortion with you forever.

Those are the three choices you will have if you get pregnant. Which would you choose?

A story I promised I'd tell . . .

I was speaking at a high school in Shreveport, Louisiana, and the auditorium was filled with teenage girls. When I finished, many of the girls in the audience came to the front to talk with me. I couldn't help but notice one girl standing to my left who seemed to be waiting for the others to leave. I can still see her face.

"Patty, I wish I could go all over the country with you and talk to teenage girls like you do," she said.

"Hey, I'd love the company," I laughed. "But why do you think you would want to do that?"

"Because I have a baby and I know what it's really like."

I put my arm around her and asked, "How old are you?"

"Fifteen," she answered.

"Are you married?"

She lowered her head as she answered, "No, he left me when I got pregnant, but I don't care."

"I'm glad to see you're still in school. Are you doing okay?"

"Yeah, I live with my parents, and my mom keeps my baby so I can come to school."

I smiled at her. She was so cute. "Well, why don't you tell me exactly what you would say to all of the teenage girls I see, and I'll tell them for you. How about that?" I asked her.

With tears brimming in her beautiful brown eyes, she said, "I'd tell them it's not worth the little bit of fun you may have because, once you get pregnant, that baby is with you 'til eternity."

Her words hit me so hard, they took my breath away. In her own simple way, she'd said it all. No matter what you do to "fix" the problem, once your body has carried another human being inside of it, that child will never, ever go away.

So there they are, the words I promised her I would tell you. They are strong and honest words from a teenage girl just like you.

Sex education and birth control . . . our hope for change?

It would be one thing if all of this pain and suffering were unavoidable and you had no control over the matter. But nothing could be further from the truth.

Pregnancy is not like cancer, it doesn't strike out of nowhere. Pregnancy is a choice, and it doesn't have to happen. Some people think the solution to this teen pregnancy problem is sex education and birth control: "Yes, that's it. Let's tell the kids all about sex, toss them a few condoms and, presto-chango, that should settle this whole mess."

I don't happen to agree with that idea. Most kids today get tons of information and education about sexual matters. Let's put it this way, you get a heck of a lot more information than any other generation of young Americans before you. You read about sex, watch it on TV, discuss it openly in health and PE classes, and view video programs covering everything from having babies to how to do it 72 ways.

I'm surprised there aren't step-by-step instructions on the back of cereal boxes. Most of you, as teens, know more about sex than your parents did when they had been married for 10 years. So, with all this constant blabbering about sex, sex, sex, is the problem getting any better? Are there fewer pregnancies than ever before? Are more teenage girls surviving their precious teen years without the heartbreak of unwanted pregnancy or abortion? NO!

And what about birth control? Anyone with an ounce of brain matter can get all of the birth control methods they want. It's to be found in nearly every store on every corner. So, again, is the problem getting any better? NO!

So, why don't these things work? Because sex education and birth control, by themselves, are not the answer. There is only one real answer to this problem and everyone seems to have overlooked it. The answer is YOU.

The knowledge that sets you free . . .

Sex education is great, as is any kind of education, because knowledge is the key to life. But, along with all of that sex education you are getting about Tab A fitting into Slot B, I think you deserve a little advice—something people my age seem to be afraid to give anymore.

You may know how to drive a car, in fact, you may have been through driver's education and had hours of instruction in the art of driving. But you became a safe and responsible driver only when you know the truth about the hazards of driving. When you realize the mind-boggling responsibility you take on every time you get behind the wheel of a car and that driving can kill you . . . that's when you become a good driver.

When you understand the truth about teen sex—how unfair it is, how few boys stay with pregnant girlfriends, what it's really like to be pregnant, how that pregnancy will change your future . . . that's when YOU start doing something about the problem. That's when YOU start saying "Not me. I'm too valuable. I want more out of life."

This is the knowledge that you need. The knowledge that sets you free.

Control and survival . . .

Let's talk about birth control. I think it's the word "control" that gets to me. I mean, is that where we are? Are we at the point where we have no "control" and must depend on something else to "control" us? Are we so weak that we can no longer make wise choices? Do we no longer have the brains or the discipline to command our own destiny? Don't you feel just a little bit insulted when, every time you turn around, somebody is handing you a free condom?

While visiting Los Angeles a while ago, I heard a senator say that he wanted to pass legislation to put an implant that will act as a birth control device in the arms of female drug users and TEENAGE GIRLS. California manages to save 100 whales every day, but during that same day, 407 California teens will drop out of school. With senators like him, I can see why they might be a little confused about what's important in life.

Then there is the genius representative from my own dear Texas who wants our state to spend $3.3 million a year giving away 1.65 million condoms to college kids.

I don't know, maybe condoms are the answer to all of life's problems. But, somehow, the thought makes me want to throw up.

Do you know why birth control doesn't work for teens? Because there hasn't been a form of birth control invented yet that doesn't require a little planning and a whole lot of discipline. No offense, but how many teens do you know who have "planning and discipline" under control in their lives? Who are we kidding, here? I personally know about three ADULTS who are big on planning and discipline—and they are all over 70. When you're young and your life becomes bogged down with a bunch of junk you aren't ready for, something usually goes wrong:

- You go on the pill, but forget to take them.
- The pill gives you nausea, so you stop taking them.
- You decide to use foam, but don't use it correctly.
- Using a condom feels too awkward or it's too much trouble.

● In the passion of the moment, no one wants to stop and take the time to put the dumb thing on. (By the way, it's not at all unusual for a boy to say he doesn't like to wear a condom because it "ruins" the feeling. Hey, if he wants to know about a ruined feeling, tell him to try having a baby.)

Look, if you *are* going to be sexually active and that's all there is to it, PLEASE, PLEASE use some sort of birth control. Don't put yourself through the heartache of a pregnancy or bring another unwanted child into this world just because you aren't willing to be honest with yourself.

A few facts: Condoms are not to be trusted when it comes to birth control - but they are the ONLY thing that will give you a chance to avoid catching a sexually transmitted disease. There are many living, breathing humans walking around today whose parents were using a condom as their choice of birth control methods. In fact, statistics tell us that 20%-30% of the times condoms are used for birth control, they fail. It's hard to believe we honestly think a thin piece of latex is the answer to some of the biggest problems our society is facing today. The truth is condoms break, they slip off, they don't get used. But they are certainly better than nothing.

Foams and gels can be very tricky because they require advance planning and the willingness to stop and use them. According to my friend, Dr. Patti Ross, pills or IUD's are probably your best bet for birth control, but you will need to go to a doctor or a clinic to get either one.

I am not going into detail about any of these birth control methods because if you want to know about birth control, there are plenty of places eager to give you all the information you could possibly use in a lifetime. Explaining birth control methods is not what this book is about.

In fact, I almost hate to write about birth control in "GIRL POWER" because I know some of you will convince yourselves that I am making suggestions here. These are NOT SUGGESTIONS! If you haven't noticed by now, I'm not pushing birth control! I'm pushing MAKING CHANGES! I'm saying: "There is a better way." I'm saying: "Be among the first generation of teenage girls to bring the teen pregnancy numbers DOWN!"

Forget about morals for the moment. Forget about what's "right" and what's "wrong". Forget about being a "bad" girl or a "good" girl. Forget about how guilty you are supposed to feel if you have sex as a teenager. None of those things are the issue here.

The issue is SURVIVAL!

YOUR survival!

Do you want to talk with me about some sort of "control?" Then, how about SELF-CONTROL? That's a subject with a future.

We know the dangers, we've changed our minds . . .

People often ask me if I seriously believe that teenage girls can bring about changes in teen pregnancy rates. They ask it like I've gone through the loop mentally. Of course, I believe in teenage girls. I believe in you with all my heart. I've talked with teenage girls like you and know that you dream of living happy lives and accomplishing your goals. I also know that you may never be able to do those things if you decide to become sexually active. But I happen to believe that if you have the opportunity to hear the honest truth about teen sex, you will make changes.

Who would have ever thought that smoking would become as unpopular as it is today? For years, the first thing anyone who wanted to look sophisticated and mature did was to stick a cigarette in his mouth. It was a status symbol. Everybody did it. Now we know that smoking is one of the dumbest things on Earth. We know what it does to your body, your health, and your future. And most of us have changed our attitudes about smoking. We won't even tolerate being in the same room with cigarette smoke. If you light up a cigarette in public these days, you may have to run for your life because more and more people are saying "We know the dangers. We understand the results. And we've changed our minds."

Someday, I believe, the very same thing will happen with teen sex. Someday, one by one, teenage girls are going to say, "We know the dangers. We understand the results. And we've changed our minds." When that day comes, you and other teenage girls will begin to take control over your own lives and own your futures, and that's something women have been *talking* about doing for a long time. Perhaps you will be the first to actually do it.

It's never too late to change your mind. You are about to read six suggestions to live by that will help you find the strength and the courage to do just that.

Listen to your mind . . .

Your mind is very powerful. It can be the best friend you will ever have. It is also quite full of good information—now that you have read this book. Now you know the realities of teen pregnancy. You know the statistics, the dangers, and the sadness.

Let your mind remember those things as you face the decision whether or not to be sexually active. Don't turn away from that voice inside of you. Don't ignore it. Let it speak to you. After all, that's YOU talking, and who knows better than YOU what's best for your life? Listen to your mind. Trust and believe in yourself.

Set your limits even before you need to . . .

The back seat of a car is not the time to have a serious discussion with yourself on how far you're going to take this thing. Decide on your limits back at home where you are not under pressure.

Remember the "peak"? All of the information you have about the peak will come in handy here because you now understand that it's easier for *you* to cool down than it is for him. So don't put yourself or your boyfriend in the position of losing control.

One of the biggest complaints guys have about us is that we start things we don't want to finish. We allow the necking and petting (those words sound so stupid) to start and, pretty soon, the guy is about to go through the roof. Then, WE decide it's time to back away. So there he sits, ready to kill somebody.

Don't play those games. It's not fair, and it may get you in more trouble than you can handle. You may have to show a little more control than the boy is willing to, so be smart enough to do just that. It's your body and your future. *You* are the one with the most to lose.

It's certainly worth a bit of planning as you face what can be one of the most serious situations of your life.

Avoid the problem . . .

If you honestly do not want to be sexually active, there are certain things that you will not do—like invite your boyfriend over when your parents are away. There is an old saying, "If you don't like the heat, stay out of the kitchen." It's an old saying, but a good one, and it means that if something is a problem, stay away from it.

Don't head for the closest "make-out" spot every chance you get. Stay away from motels, keep out of the bedrooms when you are at a party, and don't sneak him into your bedroom. When you do these things, you are creating your own worst problems. In those secluded, private, secret places, you will run into big trouble—I can promise you that.

Give yourself a break and avoid the problem.

Be ready to speak . . .

You must be ready to speak your mind when the subject of sex comes up—and it will. After all, if you can't talk honestly with him about this, what chance does this relationship have? Now that you've thought about it and know how you feel, you have to share those feelings with this boy who means so much to you. If you stammer and stutter around, your boat is on its way down. It will seem as though you haven't made a decision one way or the other. And, with your boyfriend dealing with his "peaking" problems, he will probably be more than happy to help you make a choice.

You know what you want to do, so tell him. Here are some suggestions: "I really care about you and about our relationship, but I am not ready for this." (He may ask for an estimate on when you think you might be ready. Tell him not any time soon.) "I have a lot more to lose than you do, and I'm not ready to take that chance." (Remember, it is *you* taking the chances, not him.) "I love you and I want to believe you love me, too. But when you love someone, you don't ask them to do something that could hurt them." (Or, you could ask him to prove his love for you by sticking his head in the microwave.) "What I love most about you is just simply the person you are. What do you love most about me?" (If his answer has anything to do with your body, you may have a slight problem.) "Do you understand how many teenage girls get pregnant every day and how many boys stay with a girl once she's pregnant?" (He'll swear he's different, but I wouldn't count on it.) "How do you think we would feel about each other if I got pregnant?" (His blood pressure may drop a bit on this one.) "Do you love me enough to stay with me even if we don't have sex?" (If he can't give you a firm "Yes!" you may want to ask yourself what's in this relationship for you. If you think it might be a baby, run for your life.)

Speak up. Make you voice heard!

Don't confuse "sex" with "love" ...

Females have been confusing sex with love since Moby Dick was a minnow. Sex and love are not the same thing. In fact, they are two entirely different things. They can be around at the same time or they can exist completely apart from each other. They can get along very well or they can fight constantly.

It is a natural thing to want a physically bonding relationship with the person you love. Sometimes, when your emotions are running at high tide, you almost want to crawl inside the skin of your sweetheart.

But love, the genuine kind that doesn't run away from the realities of life, never wants harm to come to its mate. True love always wants what is best for the other. When a boy really loves you, he would rather cut off his arm than bring you harm. And he'll hang in there with you no matter what. He won't throw away the relationship when he knows how strongly you feel about not getting involved in sex yet. In fact, he will support your ideals and love you even more because you have them.

You don't have to look far these days to find a girl with a sad story to tell about how a boy used her then and dumped her. I hear them every day. Sometimes, at the end of the story, the girl is pregnant, and sometimes she's not. But, always, she is brokenhearted. Usually, the stories end the same way: "But he said he loved me."

Go to the light . . .

Very few babies are made in bright daylight—but that is exactly where you can develop a great relationship. The dark may seem cozy and romantic, but it can mask the truth that you need to see.

Go to those beautiful, bright places in life where truth shines. Go on a picnic. Go bowling. Go for a nice, long walk. Go for a game of tennis. Play some golf. Go swimming. Go take a jog together. Go for a bicycle ride. Go to a concert. Take a trip to the museum. Try going to a ball game. Take a stroll around the mall. Read some poetry together under a big, oak tree. Bake a cake together. Visit your grandmother. Look at old family photos. Order a pizza. Go on a double date. Go to church. Cook dinner for him (have him bring the flowers). Play Monopoly. Sit in a library and whisper.

Spend time talking with him. Spend time doing things together. Listen to what he has to say. Listen to what he wants from life. Watch the way he acts around other people. Observe the way he treats little children. Notice how he acts when other guys show up. Watch him. Pay attention to him. Fall in love with him.

Open your eyes and see him for what he truly is. Let your relationship be flooded with light.

Why NOT wait?

When should you become sexually active? To be honest, not while you're still a teen. You may or may not agree with me. You certainly have the right to your own opinion, but it seems to me that you can't have it both ways. You will either make the decision to wait until you are older and better able to handle the consequences of a sexual relationship, or you will choose to take your chances now. There is no middle ground.

We have no problem in this country with standing up and telling teens not to do drugs. It doesn't matter if the drugs feel good, if all the kids seem to be using them, or if you might not get caught. The truth is, drugs ruin lives, so we scream and yell our heads off about them. Celebrities, educators, and politicians all jump on the band wagon against drugs. It's the popular cause to fight for.

Teen pregnancy affects many more lives than drugs do. But most of the information you get about sex only tells you how to do it without catching something. Don't let anybody kid you, when you're a teen, there is no such thing as "safe sex." That's one of the biggest lies you will ever hear. So here I am, sticking my nose in your life and saying to you, "Don't do it. Be different. Make changes." Maybe it sounds like the most stupid thing anyone could say or think these days, but I don't care.

Do you want to know when I think a teenage girl should have sex? When a pregnancy won't ruin your future or the finances of your parents. When cheerleading and slumber parties don't interest you anymore. When you can handle birth control without a slip-up. When you are ready for the 24-hour-a-day job of caring for a tiny, helpless human being. When you can take care of your child without imposing on your mother. When you know what you really want from life and make your choices based on what you believe and not what you think your boyfriend wants. When you have enough education to provide a decent future for a child. When maybe, just maybe, you think you could go through a pregnancy alone and survive.

What do you think? When do you think you might be ready for sex? I say, "Go for it," when you can handle only half of the things I just mentioned.

Until then, why not save a life?—your own.

Make a promise deep in your own heart . . .

Every 15 seconds, a female in America is beaten by her husband or boyfriend. Seven out of every 10 women who go to an emergency room with an injury have been physically abused. What does this have to do with sexual relationships with boys? Probably more than you know.

I doubt that you could find a girl anywhere who, when asked what she would like to be when she grows up, would answer, "I'd like to be abused." And, yet, that's exactly where many girls end up. How does this happen? I'll leave it to the experts to explain why men become violent, but the reason women put up with it is something we can talk about.

Women who are in abusive relationships often feel that they do not deserve to be treated any better. They have very low self-esteem. Very often they have had to get married due to pregnancy and feel desperate to have a man around to support them and their baby, so they will put up with anything because they see no way out. They have no pride in themselves, nowhere to go and no way to make a living. They feel helpless to defend themselves against a cruel husband or boyfriend, and even when their children are abused, they often sit by and do nothing.

Listen: Abusive behavior doesn't happen because a guy loves you so much he can't help himself. Sometimes we like to kid ourselves into believing such rubbish. Abusive behavior has nothing to do with love, just as rape has nothing to do with sex. Men who abuse or rape do so to show their control and power over a female. Often, they hate women.

If you have the slightest hint that the boy you are with might be physically or sexually abusive to you, get away from him as fast as you can and don't look back. Tell your parents or anyone who will listen, and don't worry about getting him into trouble. He's already in trouble—with himself. There is no future for you in such a relationship; all of his promises to "never do it again" are lies. He will do it again. And he will continue abusing until he gets professional help. In the meantime, every moment you spend with him puts you in danger. Today you still have the chance to *never* become an abused woman, but you must make the choice.

For many years, women were the property of men, so if they got out of line a bit and the man decided to rape them or slap them around, whose business was it, anyway? Well, the answer to that is that it is the business of every woman. And we must all be the ones to hold men responsible for the way they treat women and children. When men start being severely punished for crimes against women, I believe changes will come.

What can you do? Become a lawyer, a judge, or a senator and do something about the laws that go easy on abusers. Make the world a safer place for the next generation of teenage girls. And, for now, make a promise deep in your heart that no man will ever abuse you.

Today is your new beginning...

I said that you and I would go over everything I could think of on the subject of boys, and we've covered some ground together, haven't we? You've probably read a few things you would just as soon forget. I'll admit, some of it has been pretty scary. Surviving a close relationship with a boy these days is a very difficult thing to do. Many girls won't make it. The ones who do, however, will somehow learn to be strong.

It's not easy to be strong, but then it's not easy to be weak either. The results of being weak are much harder to live with. Besides that, I've found that "easy" isn't all it's cracked up to be. "Easy" doesn't give you pride in yourself. "Easy" doesn't feel good when you close your eyes at night to go to sleep. "Easy" can be very uncomfortable.

You know, the issue here is not what you have done

up to this moment in time. What matters is what you will do today. Today you can choose to follow your own heart and mind. Today you can promise to never let anyone else do your thinking for you or force you to do something you do not want to do. Today you can decide that if you lose a boyfriend you can always find another, but if you lose yourself, that can never be regained. Today you can make a vow that this is a new beginning for the most wonderful person you know—*you*!

Eight

Before we say goodbye

A long time ago, the teen years were thought to be the most fun and carefree years ever—the time when life was at its best. Then things changed. I think it had something to do with Elvis being drafted into the Army, but I'm not sure. Anyway, everything got real serious and nobody thought it was that great to be a teenager anymore.

My teen years were about as much fun as a head cold. It was probably the white skirt that did it, but that's a story for another book. All those "Beach Blanket Bingo" and "Gidget Goes Hawaiian" movies sure looked like fun, but my life never seemed that hilarious.

I don't know how you rate your teen years so far, but if you are like most girls I talk with, you're hoping it will get better from here. I know that you have to deal with a lot of stuff these days: family problems, school pressures, boyfriends, clothes, weight . . . it's all so scary. It's almost like there's a monster under your bed who's waiting for you to turn off the lights so he can jump out and get you.

Even I feel that way sometimes, and I'm old—well, older than you. It's NORMAL these days to feel frightened and afraid of other people. How sad for us all that the world is such a place.

A lot of girls I talk to are afraid. They're afraid of getting pregnant, of not finding a boyfriend, of not doing well in school, of being a failure . . . but, do you know what I've discovered? Most of our fears go away when we face them—when we just look 'em in the eye and stick our tongue out at 'em.

I never learned how to swim when I was young, and because of some frightening experiences, I became terrified of water. One day a few years ago my fabulous husband, Walter, said, "It worries me that you can't swim. I know you're afraid, but I want you to trust me. I'm going to teach you how to swim." I was 39 years old at the time and learning how to swim was not on my "Things To Do" list. But it had always bugged me that there was something in my life I was afraid of, and, I figured, if ducks could do it, why couldn't I?

As much as I feared the water, I trusted Walt more. As we walked out to the pool that afternoon, I was shaking so badly I could hardly speak. Walt smiled a lot, made me laugh and, very patiently, told me everything I needed to do. But, most important, he never let me go. In a few short moments, for the first time in my life, I swam. It was a miracle. That day, I learned three very important lessons I want to share with you before we leave each other.

Lesson #1: You have the power to change . . .

No matter what problems or fears you have today, you can overcome them. There is nothing so big or so horrible it cannot be changed. However, change will not come without a few very important actions on your part. First, you must believe YOU HAVE THE POWER TO CHANGE.

Walter could have been the greatest swimming teacher in the world, I could have had the prettiest bathing suit ever and there could have been a million-dollar prize being offered to any 39-year-old willing to jump head-first into the deep end, but none of those things were enough to make me swim—only *I* had the power to do that. And the power came from my desire to do so.

Since reading this book, are there things that you wish to change in your life? Then, *want* to! Do you have problems or fears that you wish would go away? You must *want* to find answers to them, and they will go away. Wanting to is the first step toward change.

If you have a poor relationship with your parents, do you want it to be better? Great. If you have poor self-esteem because you've never been happy with your body-picture, are you now ready to accept you and love you for what you truly are? Wonderful.

What do you want to change today? Do your friendships need some improvement? Could your relationships with boys be more balanced? Have you been sexually involved and now feel it might be smart to rethink the whole matter? When you want these things to happen, you are well on your way to making them happen.

Only you can accomplish the changes you seek.

Lesson #2: Don't be afraid to ask for help . . .

I would probably never have learned to swim if Walt hadn't shown me how. If we had walked out to the pool and he had said, "There's the water—swim," I would have run for cover. I had to have his help. When he showed me how to put my head under water and exhale through my nose, I began to see, little by little, the things I needed to do.

I asked him over and over to show me just one more time. Perhaps I was stalling a bit; the thought of putting my head under the water was less than thrilling, I can promise you. But each time he showed me and told me that I could do it, my fears became smaller and my determination greater. "Sure, I can do it," I began to believe.

When something needs to be fixed in your life, don't be afraid to ask for help. None of us have all of the answers to all of our problems all of the time, and you should be suspicious of people who say they do. Who can you talk to today about your problems and fears? Who in your life do you know you can trust?

I wish every teenage girl in the world had a "granny", some older person who loves and cares for young people and will listen and be sympathetic, but tell you what you need to hear, even when you don't want to hear it. My granny is gone now, but there have been other, very special women in my life who have given me strength and guidance. Maybe there is a "granny" somewhere in your life. Maybe she's a neighbor or a teacher or an aunt. Whomever you choose to tell your secrets to, stay close to them and never be afraid to ask for help.

Lesson #3: Don't let go of each other . . .

I can still feel Walt's arms holding me up as I found myself surrounded by all of that water. Even when I attempted to go it alone, I knew his arms weren't very far away. If he had let go of me and told me to do it by myself, I'm not sure what would have happened. Perhaps I would have still learned to swim, but it would have been much harder.

A few years ago, my daughter Hilary and her good friends, Cheryl and Eileen, planned a three-day trip to Galveston, Texas, for spring break. Their room was reserved, their bags were packed, and they were all set for some fun in the sun. I was trying my best not to be a typical mother during all of the planning. "After all," I kept telling myself, "it's Hilary's senior year and it's time for her to do these things. I trust her, and I trust Eileen and Cheryl. I know they'll be fine." But deep in my heart, I was worried that something might go wrong.

The day before they were to leave, I told the girls that I wanted to see them before they left. They agreed to meet at our house at noon. Seated around the kitchen table, I looked at the faces of those three precious girls and said, "You are starting out on an exciting journey, but there are dangers out there. Stick together, watch out for each other, protect each other, and you will be fine." We held hands, said a little prayer, and they were off. They had a wonderful time!

Well, it is time for *us* to do what the boys have been doing for a long time. It is time for us to stick together, watch out for each other and protect each other.

Yes, it can be quite a challenge to travel this road called "change." And the dangers along the way are very real. But, if you will believe in yourself and the power you possess and hold on to each other, I know that you will make it.

I will say good-bye for now. Be safe. And . . . God, please bless the teenage girls.

Appendix

Survey

Approximately 7,000 girls throughout the United States, ages 13-18, responded to the following survey during the period of September 1989 through May 1992.

1. If you could change one thing about yourself, what would it be?

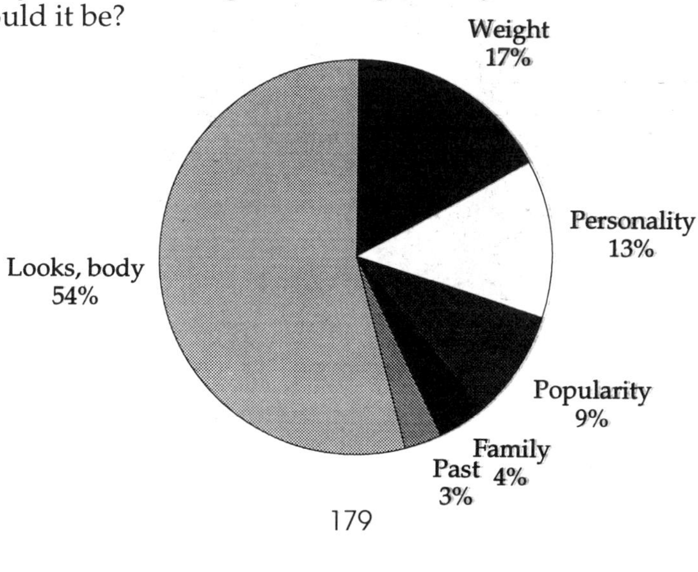

2. What is your biggest fear?

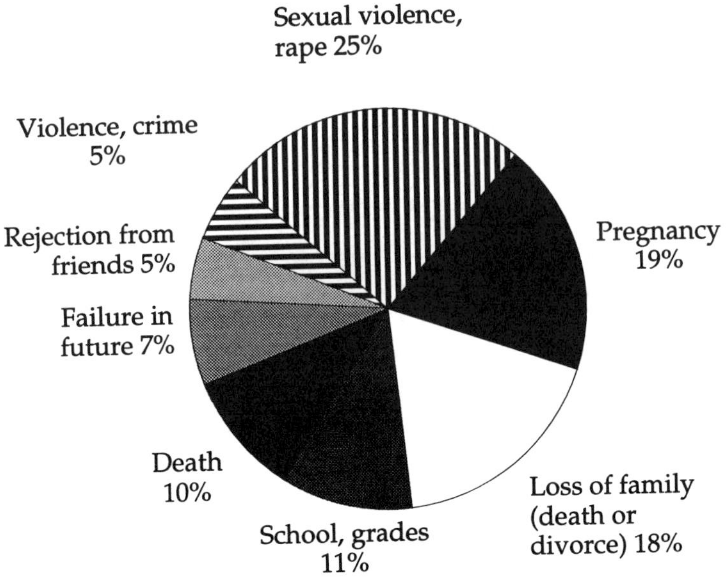

3. What person do you admire most?

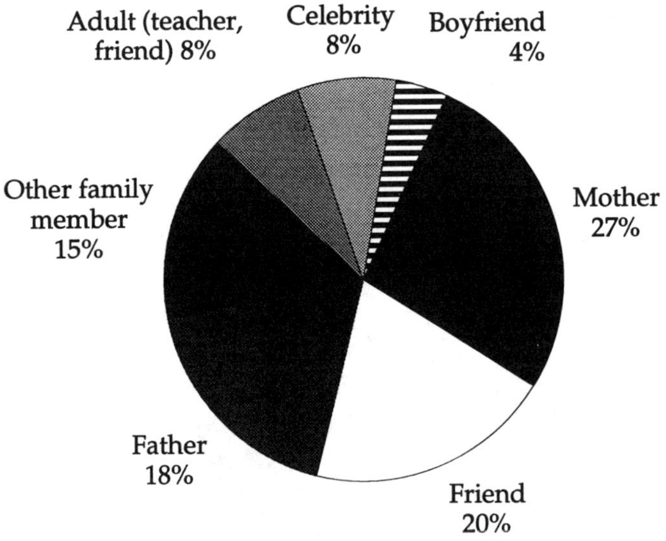

4. Have you ever experienced sexual abuse . . .

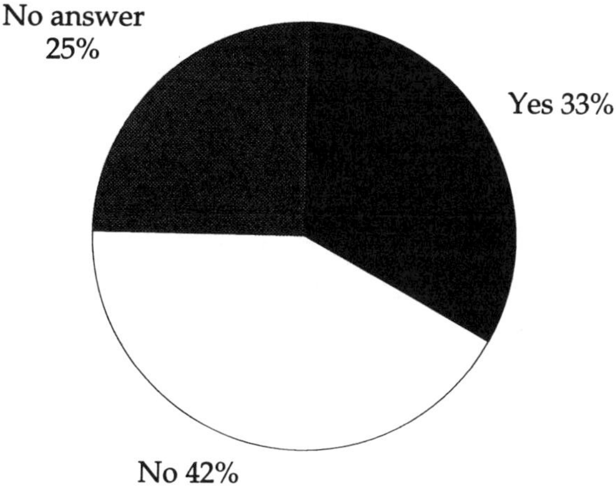

Have you ever experienced physical abuse . . .

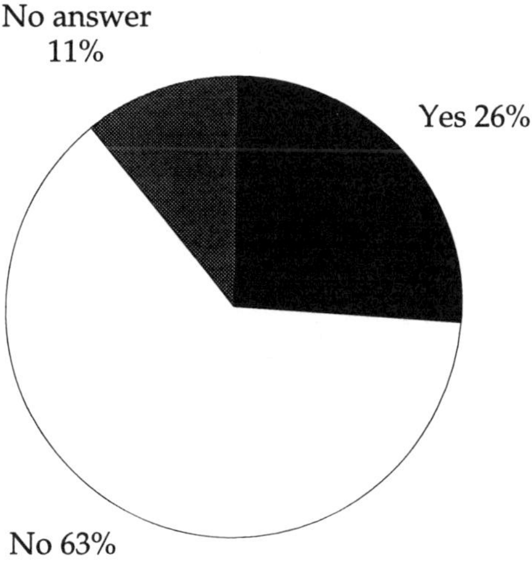

If you have experienced any kind of abuse, did you tell someone . . .

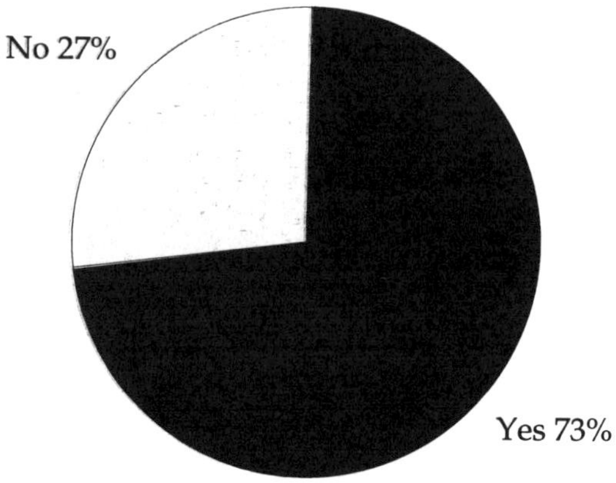

5. Would you change anything about your family and, if so, what would it be?

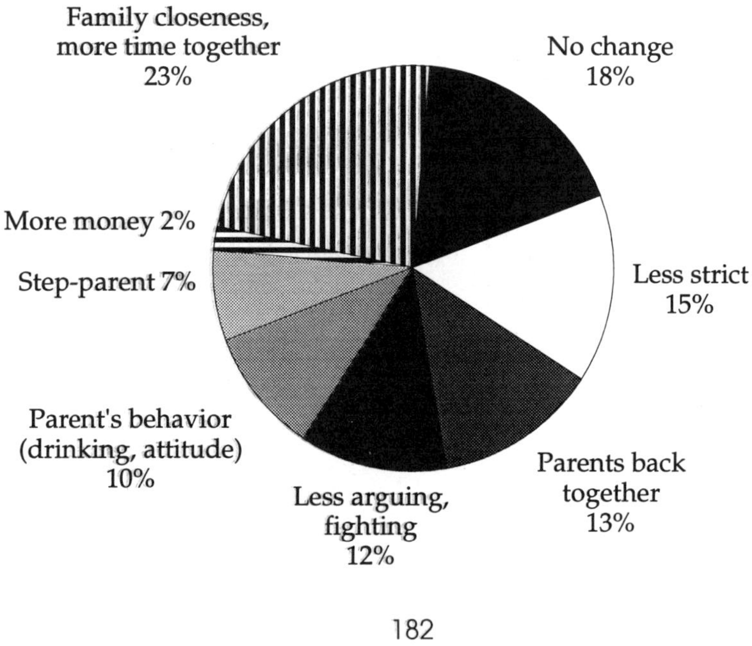

6. Do you believe there is more drug or alcohol abuse among teens today?

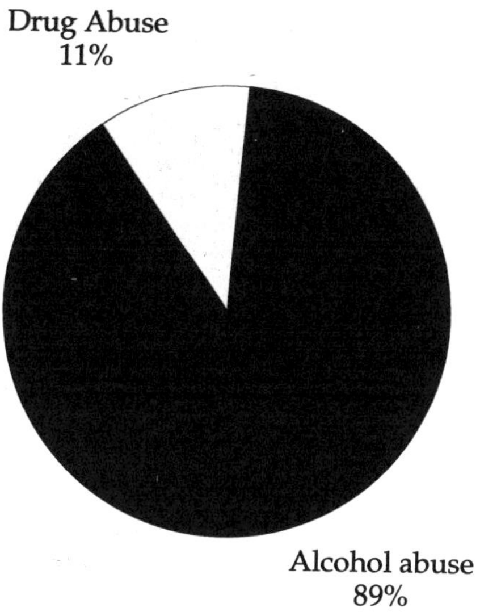

7. How much time do you watch TV each day?

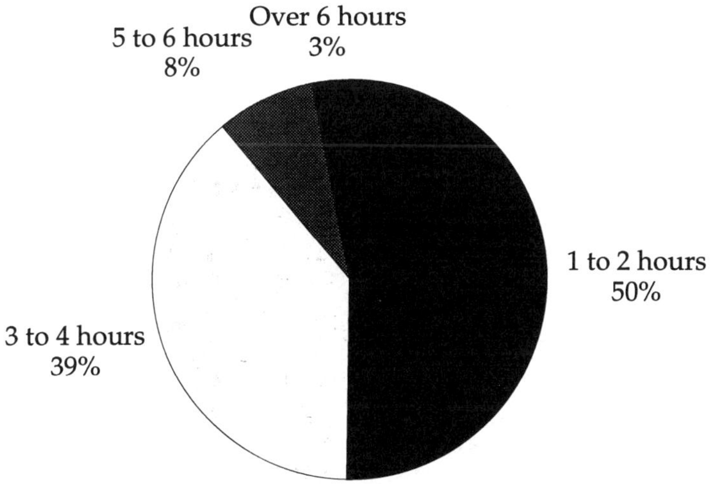

8. How many movies (at home or at the cinema), do you watch each week?

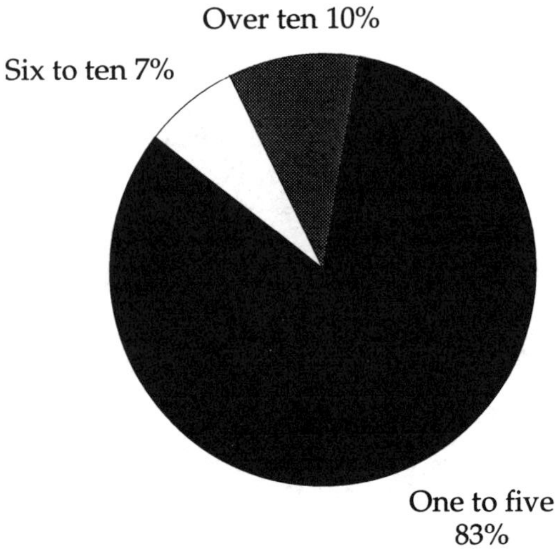

9. How do you feel most rock and rap videos portray females?

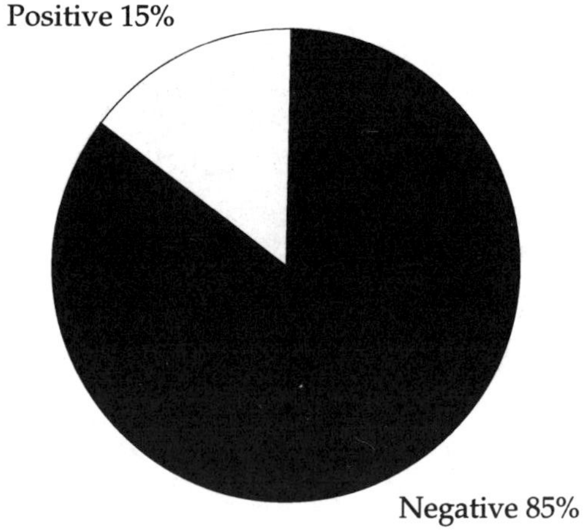

10. What is the first thing you look for in a boy?

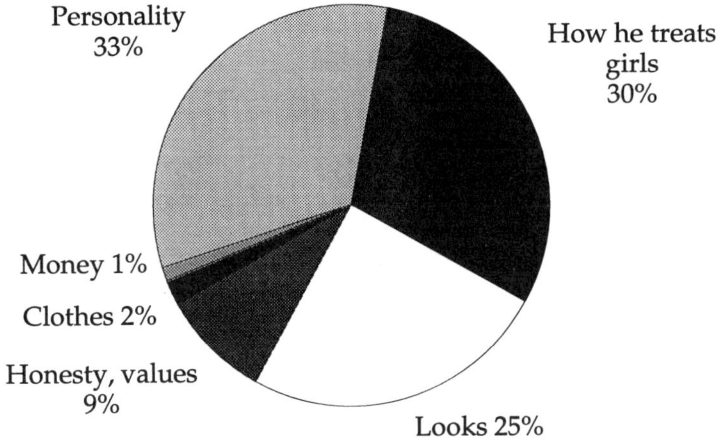

11. Which of the following best describes why most girls choose to become sexually active . . .

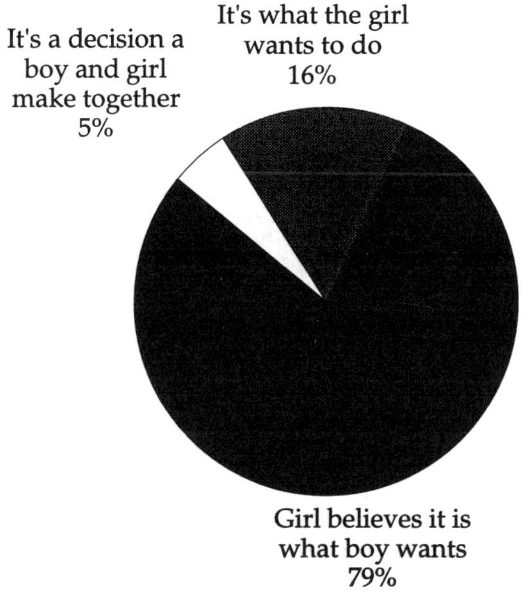

12. What do you expect to be doing when you are 35 years old?

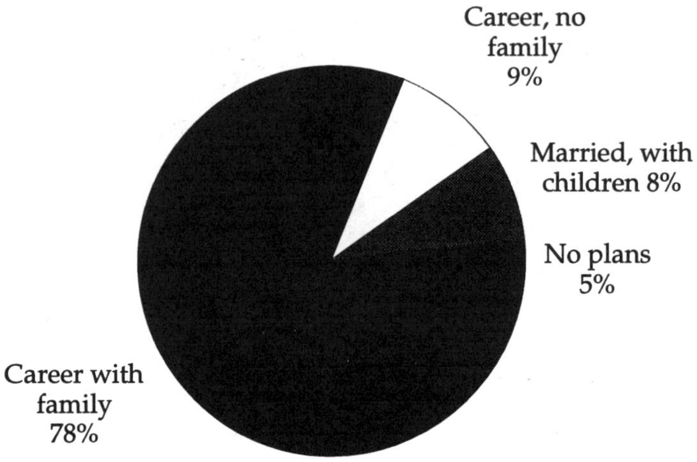

13. What is the biggest problem in your life?

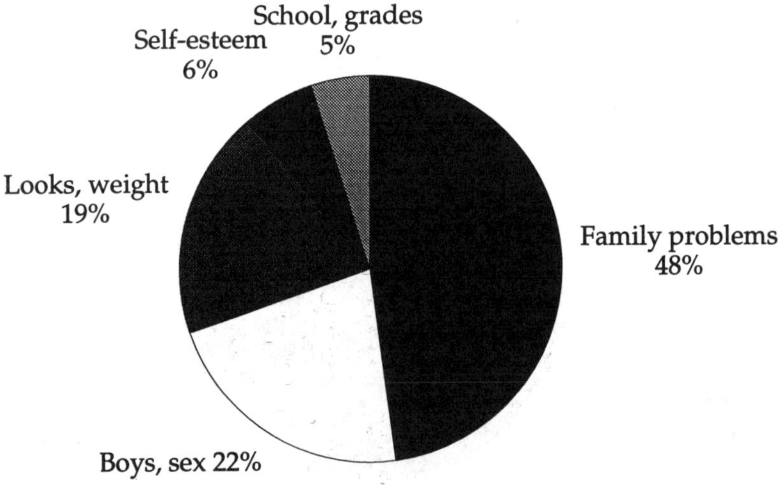

14. What makes you the happiest?

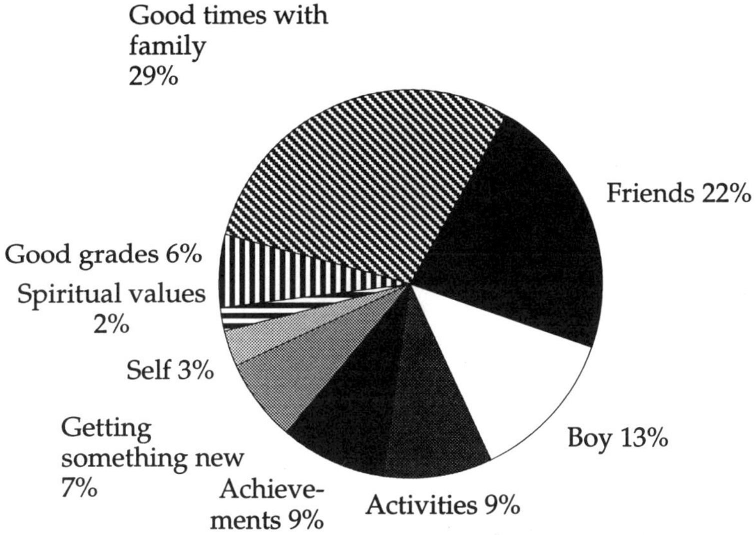

15. Most of the time, do you think of yourself as a happy person?

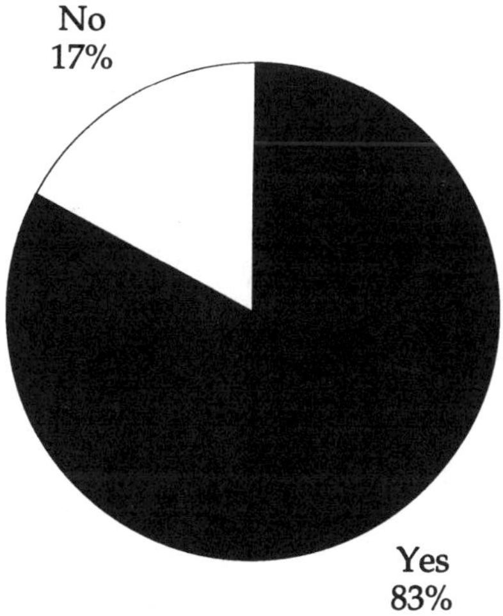